What others are saying about
SEVEN FOODS OF TH

We all eat every day, all day, so learning a deeper meaning of food from a more heavenly perspective seems wise. *7 Foods of the Promised Land* is a beautiful weaving of nutrition, history, recipes, and the Bible that sets the table for sweet fellowship with our Creator.

Pam Farrel, author of 59 books including bestselling *Men Are Like Waffles, Women Are Like Spaghetti* and coauthor of *Discovering Hope in the Psalms: A Creative Bible Study Experience*

Annette has created the definitive reference for the foods of the Bible in this insightful and thoroughly researched book. A unique work on nutrition that links science to Scripture as the restorative properties of the foods identified in the Bible are explored. From the pomegranate to kernels of wheat, Annette details the seven species of Israel in this insightful and well researched work that links science to scripture in a journey of restoration and redemption. It is really an amazing read. The Hebraic perspectives that Annette brings out will help the church recover what has been lost.

Dr Mark Jenkins, Director of Hope For Israel USA, founding member of the Jerusalem Prayer Breakfast, former US representative for the Christian desk of Yad Vashem and Associate pastor of Berea Baptist Church.

Annette's book, *The Seven foods of the Promised Land*, is amazing. She does an excellent job of not only explaining how each of the seven foods are meant to remind us of God's promises and provisions but she also shares the amazing health benefits of each food. I highly encourage everyone to read it.

Rhonda Carroll, Coach, Biblical Nutrition Academy Inner Circle

As a pastor, I greatly enjoyed reading Annette's book, *The Seven Foods of the Promised Land*." She gives inspiration into how these seven foods are such great reminders of the powerful promises given from God. This book will not only bless you with the reminders of the amazing things God has done for us, but it will also give you the reasons as to why these foods are so important for our overall health.

Jake Carroll, B.Ministry; MBA, Th.D,
Pastor Abba's House

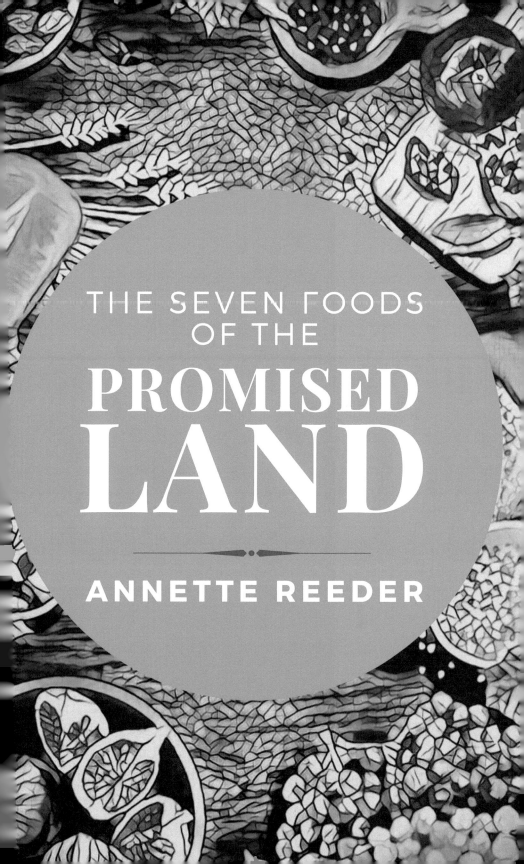

THE SEVEN FOODS OF THE

PROMISED LAND

ANNETTE REEDER

THE SEVEN FOODS OF

THE

PROMISED LAND

Annette Reeder

Bold Vision Books
PO Box 2011
Friendswood, TX 77549

Copyright ©Annette Reeder 2023
ISBN 978-1-946708-89-2
Library of Congress Control Number 2023935341
All rights reserved.
Published by Bold Vision Books, PO Box 2011, Friendswood, Texas 77549 www.
boldvisionbooks.com

Cover and Interior Art by Emily Wiegand
Cover Design by Amber Wiegand-Buckley
Interior design by kae Creative Solutions

Published in the United States of America.

DEDICATION

These are the *bubele* (Hebrew for loved ones) who led to the desire to see this book in your hands today.

My mom, the mission master. She taught me how to see the world through a biblical mission worldview with the end goal in mind – be on the mission God has called you.

No evangelist or missionary was within fifty miles of our home without being invited to our home and dinner table. She desired for each of us to hear how God was at work in all parts of the world. She instilled in me the love of cooking and the desire to always be on mission. She was a *balaboosta* (Hebrew for excellent homemaker).

My dad, the sheltering servant. He is a *bubele.* After mom went to heaven, my dad took us on our first journey to Israel. The trip answered many questions from my reading of the Bible. And it sparked many more. This trip ignited my desire as the Biblical Nutritionist to bring the history of the land together with the flavors of Jerusalem.

Then most of all, my husband Steve, the patient provider, my *mechaieh* (Hebrew for a real joy or pleasure). He has excitedly packed his bags to travel with me across the oceans to see sugar cane fields in Hawaii, chocolate trees in the Caribbean, or St. Peter's fish from the Sea of Galilee. Without his patience and provisions what you see in this book would have never flowed through my keyboard.

TABLE OF CONTENTS

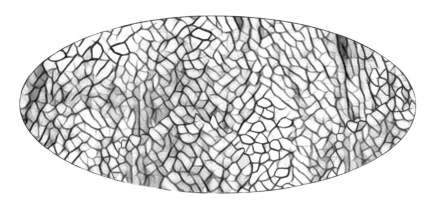

INTRODUCTION

My husband and I led a short-term youth mission trip to Romania. Our days were spent in dry heat, sharing the Gospel with kids and playing kickball on the powdery dirt fields. In the evening, we were greeted with an ice cold soda called Fanta™. Everyone was immediately captivated by it. We'd never tasted such refreshment. How humorous it was to come back to the states and find Fanta soda in the local market.

On our first trip to Israel, falafel captivated us. This delicious bean croquette is served as a main course, a side vegetable, or piled into a pita with lettuce, tomatoes, and a delicious tzatziki sauce. It was on the menu for breakfast, lunch, and dinner every day of our tour. I never tired of it, but my husband never wanted to see another falafel again.

Today my senses connect the discovery of these foods to God's workings in and around us.

Seeing Fanta soda reminds me of our trip to Romania. God provided the words to share, guided us through difficult transportation issues, and opened up opportunities to reach people who seemed eager to hear the Gospel.

When I enjoy falafel, my senses take me back to the stone streets in Israel and our mission to plant a biblical foods garden in the city of Jerusalem. You can read more about this experience in Part 2 of this book.

In Jerusalem, God led us to the specific places where he is at work today in the lives of His people. He brought us through customs with few questions of our assignment, and he taught us how to pray fervently for the people of Israel.

Foods can be the initiating reminder of God's promises, provisions, and grace.

FOOD STIRS UP THE FLAVORS OF GRACE

God intended the same for the Israelites. He placed reminders in places such as Egypt and in ceremonies such as the Passover Lamb to be an annual reminder of His saving grace for the righteous. Just a sip of water on a hot and dry day was a reminder of the water God supplied in the wilderness just three days after parting the Red Sea. Noah and his family were saved from the catastrophic world-wide flood. Jonah was given a second chance to reach the people of Nineveh. Reminders continue throughout the Old and New Testament. Each reminder is a complete covenant of God's perfect story of grace. It is a continual reminder of his promises, provisions, and grace. Food in Scripture is used for these reminders and lessons of His grace.

During the spring Passover feast, Jewish families and now numerous Christians enjoy delicious foods, which help to retell the story of deliverance. Lamb is served as a reminder of the Lamb of God who takes away the sins of the world. Bitter herbs are added to be a reminder of the hard labor experienced in captivity. And my favorite is unleavened bread. This is a flat bread with no yeast. Removing the leaven (yeast) from the entire home is a fun activity for the kids as an annual reminder to remove all sin from our lives and to be a blessing to the Lord. Food is used by God to be reminders of his promises, provisions, and grace. Are you noticing a theme? We all need reminders of God fulfilling His promises. We need reminders of how he provides. And we need daily reminders of His grace.

PROMISES

God's Word is written for us today. The Bible is about the promise of redemption through Jesus Christ, our Yeshua Messiah. The thread woven in every word, every happening, and every teaching will always draw tight the reminder of God's promises. Abraham understood God's promises.

> *With respect to the promises of God, he did not waver in unbelief, but grew strong in faith, giving glory to God* (Romans 4:20 NASB).

The promise given to him yet revealed to all of us. God promised. God fulfilled. God still promises. God will fulfill. We too, can lean on His promises.

PROVISIONS

God provides today just as he did in ancient times. And food is a daily example.

> *Do not worry then, saying, "What shall we eat?" or "What shall we drink?" or "What are we to wear for clothing?" For the Gentiles eagerly seek all these things; for your heavenly Father knows that you need all these things* (Matthew 6:31-32 NASB).

> *And my God shall supply all your needs according to His riches in glory in Christ Jesus* (Philippians 4:19 NASB).

God provided. He still provides, and he will always provide.

GRACE

Grace is like the cinnamon topping on the muffin. Underserved yet, graciously accepted. The common definition of grace is: "God's life, power and righteousness given to us by unmerited favor." Unmerited favor, and I am so glad of this. We don't deserve it. Just like the Israelites, we complain and seek other ways. Yet, God works effectively in our hearts to change lives for good. Grace gives us a new life which is not condemned by God. When we get to heaven, there will be joyful streams of tears flowing from our hearts when we see how truly gracious and loving our Father is by the gift of grace. Grace offered and grace received to those in the Old Testament and in the New Testament. Grace offered to us and grace received by us continually.

Food, a daily necessity, is a pictorial menu of these promises, provisions, and grace.

What is your favorite food from childhood? What memories come to mind when you eat that totally revered food? My favorites include a banana split birthday cake when I was nine. And my aunt's double chocolate chip cookies, which were served at the family farm where I played in the barn and smelled like hay for the next three days. What food stirs delicious memories for you?

My husband loves lasagna, and I remember the best lasagna meal we enjoyed together. It was our first month wedding anniversary, and we ate at Del Pietro's On the Hill in St. Louis. It was the best hot bubbly, oozy, cheesy mouth watering lasagna ever. Every time I think of lasagna today, I remember the floor to ceiling glass windows overlooking the twinkling city lights and sharing time with my new love.

Now let's take our imaginations on a trip back in history. It is the year 1350 BC and we are sitting at the family dinner table along the shores of Galilee. Grandfather is retelling about the days of walking in the desert until they reached the Promised Land. Listen as he speaks.

"Each night we reclined for our dinner of manna and quail AGAIN—the only food I'd ever experienced. My parents talked incessantly about how they missed the leeks, onions, garlic, and cucumbers. My father would purse his lips in a kiss to his fingers as he named each vegetable. He recalled every detail of the food: how it felt in his hands, the aroma when the vegetables were sliced, and especially the unique potent flavor. I assumed these foods must be the sweetest foods on earth. Glory be to heaven. I was surprised when I bit into a raw garlic clove the first time.

Whoa – what were they thinking?"

Food evokes memories, and memories are a reminder of God's grace.

Manna and quail in the wilderness remind us how God provides. The wilderness was the perfect place for God to show how he provides, which is the answer to the promise where God revealed how much he loved His own. Through all the struggles and disbelief, God also revealed His grace. Without the showing of grace no one would have entered the Promised Land. The story would have ended there. Yet, God never goes against his word.

Fanta soda revives the abundant joy of living and serving God in Romania.

Falafel brings back all the memories of the sights and sounds of Israel. The land God calls home.

All flavors of God's grace. All reminders of His provisions and promises.

THE ISRAELITES EXPERIENCE GRACE

In Deuteronomy, two specific examples help us understand more about grace. The book of Deuteronomy is the pinnacle of love and loyalty. Most people when questioned about love in the Bible will turn to 1 Corinthians 13, the love chapter. Yet, the longest love story written is in Deuteronomy. In this book Moses speaks the words of the Lord to forewarn and bless God's chosen people. Dangers await, distractions are abounding, and decisions will need to be premeditated. The most loving parent will train a child well to be on guard for danger and how to prepare and overcome. As a loving parent, God prepares us.

An early example of his grace is food. He provides seven specific foods.

> For the LORD your God is bringing you into a good land, a land of streams of water, of fountains and springs, flowing out in valleys and hills; a land of wheat and barley, of vines, fig trees, and pomegranates, a land of olive oil and honey; a land where you will eat food without shortage, in which you will not lack anything; a land whose stones are iron, and out of whose hills you can dig copper. When you have eaten and are satisfied, you shall bless the LORD your God for the good land which He has given you. (Deuteronomy 8:7-10 NASB).

The seven species, Shiv'at HaMinim in Hebrew, of the Promised Land are not just random foods. They are specific. Even the listing of the seven is significant. The seven foods are listed in order of their ripening. Wheat and barley are first in the spring. Vines, fig trees and pomegranates ripen in late summer, and olives and dates are last in the fall. These foods were identified specifically for the Israelites for revelation of promises, provisions, and grace. They are also for us today to learn the same.

The second example—which we will cover in amazing detail later—is why God chose those specific foods. Knowing God's *why* is going to incite a new love for our Lord and how he continues to reveal His promises, provisions, and grace.

But first let's take a look at the foods. In the eighth chapter of Deuteronomy, Moses recounts everything God has miraculously done. Moses does not want the people to forget the journey and therefore squander the promises. The entire book of Deuteronomy is a love letter spoken by Moses to the people from a God who desires to see his people enter the Promised Land.

All the commandments that I am commanding you today you shall be careful to do, that you may live and multiply, and go in and possess the land which the Lord swore to give your forefathers. [promised] *And you shall remember all the way which the Lord your God has led you in the wilderness these forty years* [provided], *that He might humble you, testing you, to know what was in your heart, whether you would keep His commandments or not. And He humbled you and let you be hungry, and fed you with manna* [provided] *which you did not know, nor did your fathers know, that He might make you understand that man does not live by bread alone, but man lives by everything that proceeds out of the mouth of the Lord* [grace].

For the LORD your God is bringing you into a good land, a land of brooks of water, of fountains and spring, flowing forth in valleys and hills. [promised, provided, grace]. (Deuteronomy 8:1-3, 7 NASB bracketed words mine).

He wanted their attention, and he needed to give last minute reminders. Soon he would send them into battle to possess the land promised hundreds of years ago to Abram in Genesis 12. Entering the Promised Land was supposed to be a short journey. It became a long forty-year journey. It was the highlight of a long awaited promise.

Moses' words claimed their attention because they'd never seen nor tasted the food he described. Yet these foods must be amazing because Moses concluded his speech by saying, "When you have eaten and are satisfied, you shall bless the Lord your God for the good land which he has given you" (Deuteronomy 8:10 NASB).

Imagine food so good you will praise God for it.

After years of wandering, God delighted the taste buds of the Israelites with a delicious banquet. Food that satisfies both spiritually and physically. Today science has proven the spiritual and physical connection. Saying and believing the words *God loves me* and *God cares for me* has been proven to change your physical immune response. Just the belief in those words increases the T-cell count in your body. T-cells, lymphocyte cells, are the immune system being called into action. against invaders. They are made from stem cells and are highly effective against cancer cells and HIV. The spiritual affects the physical. Yet, it is the physical stem cells that create the stem cells. And the longevity of the stem cells is highly influenced by beliefs. The physical affects the spiritual. If your body was under attack, would you want a large army fighting for you? I would. And when we declare agreement with our heart and mind by saying, "God loves me," we muster an army of cells. So when Moses wrote, "When you have eaten and are satisfied, you shall bless the Lord your God," he is saying we have an opportunity to declare God loves me. The Israelites were never aware of how their praises were boosting their immune system. God was. Moses may have not understood the fullness of these words. God knew.

When they crossed into the Promised Land, the Israelites enjoyed fruit from orchards they did not plant. Food from ground they did not turn over.

My husband has dreamed since we first married to live in a lake house for our permanent home, so he occasionally talks about moving. I always cringe at the thought because I have worked hard at improving my yard with garden beds and an orchard, including plums, peaches, apples, figs, pomegranates, blueberries, and strawberries. And this past year we built a cute Johanna Gaines stylish greenhouse. I don't want to start over. For me to want to move to a new home, it must have an orchard, garden, and perhaps a greenhouse. Just like the Israelites, I want the yard and garden move-in ready.

God gave the Israelites a prepared banquet feast ready for the plucking and enjoying. God had been cultivating these nutrient rich foods since the family of 70 people left for Egypt more than 440 years earlier. These seven foods will delight the palate, invigorate the cells, and rejuvenate stamina.

Plus, they are a continual reminder of his grace. Adam and Eve were placed in a move-in ready garden and instructed to enjoy its bounty. Now the Israelites are set up to relish fellowship with the Lord and enjoy the Promised Land. Although unlike Adam and Eve, the Israelites will have to work to gain control over the land. Yet, the promise is still there, God will go before us, and God will never leave us or forsake us.

Every meal, every season and every feast became continual reminders of His grace. God's design. God's purpose in creation. Remember this is just the introduction. Wait till you read in Part 2 why God chose these 7 foods. I can hardly wait till you get there. But don't skip Part 1 where you will discover more about these amazing foods.

PART 1

7 FOODS WITH 7 REMINDERS

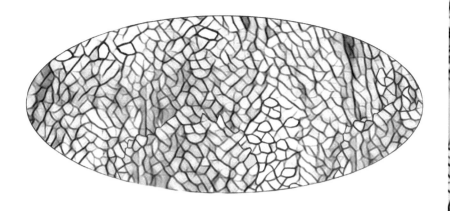

GROCERY AISLES OF SCRIPTURE

Let's walk the grocery aisles of Scripture and discover for ourselves why these seven foods are cell stirring. Why did God choose these specific foods? What is the significance of relating these foods to him? The answers will delight your heart and satisfy your cravings.

We will discover nutrition facts that would make any supplement company envious. And overall, we will see the hand of God. He connects us with nourishing and satisfying foods today as He did for His chosen people many years ago.

Each of these foods imparts a blessing. They are each so unique, yet complement one another in texture, color, and flavor. Wheat is soft and sweet, and barley is tough and hard. Grapes are succulent and deliciously juicy, and figs are plump and fleshy, while pomegranates are tangy, vibrant and crunchy. The bitterness of the olives contrasts the perfect honeyed sweetness of the dates.

If your spiritual and physical appetite is ready, then get your grocery lists ready and open your prayer journal. What you are about to learn is going to tempt your palate at every meal.

We start with identifying the seven foods of the Promised Land, which are normally referred to as the Seven Species. I will share their nutrition benefits, especially since that is my degree of study. But don't miss Part 2 where I unveil the spiritual significance of why God chose these seven. It was an incredible heart beat in my study and I hope in yours as well.

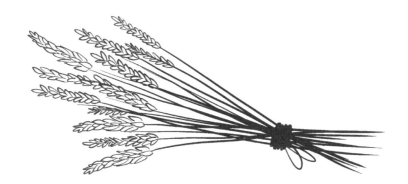

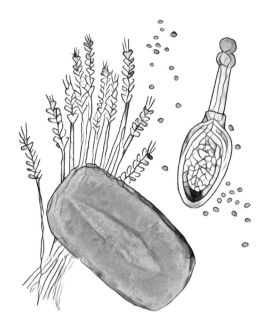

WHEAT

"He would feed him with the finest of wheat and with honey out of the rock I will satisfy you" (Psalm 81:17).

"For we have stores of wheat, barley, oil, and honey hidden in the field" (Jeremiah 41:8).

"No one shall take a handmill or an upper millstone in pledge, for he would be taking a life in pledge." (Deuteronomy 24:6).

Wheat is a staple in life from the beginning of Genesis to the end of Revelation. Wheat is mentioned 50 times in the Bible, while bread is mentioned more than 400 times. Its value made it a treasure worth hiding and safekeeping. It is the crop of life, and the millstone represents a person's livelihood. Wheat made the difference between life and death because of its nutritional value and the protection it offered against a host of disabling and often deadly disorders and diseases.

WHEAT IN THE BIBLE

Wheat ripened around the time of Pentecost. Just as barley was offered to God on the first day of the week after Passover, so also was wheat offered on Pentecost seven weeks later.

> *You shall celebrate the Feast of Weeks, that is, the first fruits of the wheat harvest, and the Feast of Ingathering at the turn of the year* (Exodus 34:22 NASB).

God provided wheat and other grains for the purpose of communion bread. Communion with him. When Jesus was tempted by Satan in the wilderness (Matthew 4:1-4), he quoted Deuteronomy (8:1-4) and kept communion with the Lord God. Satan desired to break the promises of God by having Jesus turn to him just as Eve did in the garden. This temptation followed his 40 day fast. He was hungry. Isn't it interesting that the first temptation is food for both Eve and Jesus? You may believe you are the only person tempted by food in the middle of a time of worship or life's challenges. Consider also how the Israelites were always complaining how their hunger was overwhelming them. They begged Moses to find food. And God provided. The plan for the Israelites was to spend a short time in the desert, experience the presence of the Lord, and then move into the garden of the Promised Land. That didn't happen. It took 40 years. In Matthew 4, Jesus took the same short journey, but he didn't fail. Jesus entered the presence of God in the wilderness, and as he ended his fast and was ready to be revealed as the Promised One, Satan jumped at the opportunity to dissuade.

WHEAT AS FOOD DURING BIBLICAL DAYS

In biblical days, wheat or other grains would be served with every meal. Even toasted wheat kernels could travel for days in a warrior's pouch. (For us today this is the new popcorn! See my recipe in Part 3 of this book.)

Remember the story in Matthew 12:1 when Jesus' disciples became hungry and began to pick the heads of grain and eat? God provided, even though the Pharisees criticized.

Another account of God's grace and provision is an event with the prophet Ezekiel.

> *But as for you, take wheat, barley, beans, lentils, millet, and spelt, put them in one vessel and make them into bread for yourself* (Ezekiel 4:9 NASB).

Wheat was enjoyed daily. It was the staple and satisfying element of the diet. It gave them energy for daily work and fiber for daily cleansing. Fiber is one of the most critical nutrients for protection in the body against disease. Did they know this nutritional fact in the biblical days? No. All they knew was grain, specifically wheat, was a food that satisfies. This satisfaction is an example of His grace. Always satisfying.

GREAT GRAIN ROBBERY

Jesus is the bread of life.

> *I am the bread of life. He who comes to me shall never hunger, and he who believes in me shall never thirst* (John 6:35 ESV).

> *I am the living bread which came down from heaven. If anyone eats of this bread, he will live forever; and the bread that I shall give is My flesh, which I shall give for the life of the world* (John 6:51 NKJV).

Joyce Rogers, wife of the late Dr. Adrian Rogers, wrote in her book, *The Bible's Seven Secrets to Healthy Eating*, about the great grain robbery. This title fits. A century ago, man developed the ability to separate the wheat flour from the life of the wheat berry—the germ and fiber. This process removed more than 26 nutrients, plus the bran (fiber). When this manipulation of the wheat spread through society, the need for sanitariums rose across the country as more and more people were mentally challenged with Beri-Beri and Pellagra—a mind altering B vitamin deficiency. Bread was no longer life sustaining. It was an altered food missing the key life-giving elements.

DNA OF WHEAT

Have you ever wondered about the DNA in the food you eat? DNA is within every living organism in God's creation. It is in the body, plants, animals, and yes, the food served on the table. Food like fresh fruits, vegetables, grains, bread, and so on. So what is the importance of even paying attention and understanding food's DNA?

God designed DNA to self-replicate. With this genetic code, humans reproduce humans, animals reproduce animals, and plants reproduce plants. What's fascinating is that DNA was once thought to be a spiral ladder of Junk DNA (yes, that is the scientific term), but it's now realized to be far more complex. There's so much wisdom and intricacy in the DNA.

DNA has revealed God's masterpiece. His fingerprints on creation.

Scientists today are having a hard time denying the perfect design by an intelligent creator. Within Scriptures, we know God had a master plan for his perfect creation. Focus on the DNA within food helps us see how perfect God's design really is. Not only is God's message and love for us reflected on the outside of his creation, what we see and touch, but also from deep within.

For years—decades really—man has been working studiously to understand microscopically the DNA of food. A whole process comes with understanding food's DNA. The scientific mindset is: Learn the DNA>Change the DNA>Control the crops>Control the food>Control the people. When the DNA was deciphered, scientists began genetically modifying the organism (GMO). We see these altered foods in the grocery stores and at the dinner table. The understanding or value of GMO (genetically modified organism) foods cause people to be polar opposites in their beliefs of whether this intervention is good or bad. In 2002, scientists decoded the genome, (genetic material—DNA) of rice. In 2008, they completed the genome of soybeans. In 2009, they mapped the maize (corn) genome. Then it was time for wheat. Wheat studies were complicated and the answers evasive. Scientists say wheat is arguably the most critical crop in the world. It is grown on more land than anything else (even without man's intervention). Wheat provides humanity with a fifth of our calories. It is in your bread, your pastry, and your pasta. Truth be told, wheat is an important crop – both biblically and politically.[1]

Some verses from the Bible talk about the significance of bread and how Jesus considered himself as the "bread of life."

"I am the living bread that came down out of heaven; if anyone eats of this bread, he will live forever; and the bread also which I will give for the life of the world is My flesh" (John 6:51 NASB).

Jesus said to them, "I am the bread of life; he who comes to Me will not hunger, and he who believes in Me will never be thirsty" (John 6:35 NASB).

"I am the bread of life" (John 6:48 NASB).

"Now He who supplies seed to the sower and bread for food will supply and multiply your seed for sowing and increase the harvest of your righteousness" (2 Corinthians 9:10 NASB).

Why did our Lord compare himself to the bread of life? Most importantly, what exactly does this statement mean? As it turns out, there's a deep and beautiful message to be found. To no surprise, it comes right down to the very DNA.

While the genome of *Arabidopsis*—the first plant to be sequenced—contains 135 million DNA letters, and the human genome contains 3 billion, bread wheat has *16 billion*. Yes, you read that correctly,

16 billion. More genome is in wheat than in people. Just one of wheat's chromosomes—3B—is bigger than the entire soybean genome. Scientists (and perhaps politicians) have wanted control over wheat since DNA and GMO first surfaced. With the knowledge of the DNA in crops, scientists are able to create new varieties that are claimed to be more herbicide resistant and drought tolerant. This is science trying to improve on God's creation. Not possible!

To make things more incredible to me as a Bible believer, the bread-wheat genome is really **three completely different genomes in one**. In science lingo, that's a hexaploid genome. In simpler terms, it's a revelation of the One who creates. Jesus is the Bread of Life and in him we see the Father and the Holy Spirit. The complexity of this discovery is why wheat has not been able to be modified until recently. Praise the Lord. God reveals his intricacies in the bread of life.

Now, if that doesn't butter your bread, your toaster is broken.

SPIRITUAL SIGNIFICANCE OF WHEAT

Why do you spend your money for what is not bread and your wages for what does not satisfy? Listen carefully to Me, and eat what is good, and delight yourself in abundance (Isaiah 55:2 NASB).

Give us this day our daily bread (Matthew 6:11 NASB).

And they were continually devoting themselves to the apostles' teaching, and to fellowship, to the breaking of bread and to prayer (Acts 2:42 NASB).

I will abundantly bless her provision; I will bless her needy with bread (Psalms 132:15 NASB1995).

No man shall take a handmill or an upper millstone in pledge, for he would be taking a life in pledge. (Deuteronomy 24:6 NASB1995).

These verses illustrate the continual importance of bread. Jesus loved having others break bread with him. Those were moments of blessing, intimacy, and revelation. Jesus broke bread with those on the road to Emmaus and their spiritual eyes were opened to know him. He broke bread with the disciples at the Passover and revealed the meaning of His death. After His resurrection, Jesus broke bread with the disciples and fellowshipped with them as they had breakfast together by the sea. In the Book of Revelation, Jesus invited the lukewarm Christians to break bread with him and allow their hearts to be rekindled by the fire of his love. He intended for us to break bread with him on a daily basis.

SEEDS WITH PHYSICAL BENEFITS

As noted in my books *Healthy Treasures Cookbook* and *Treasures of Healthy Living Nutrition Manual,* wheat berries, fully intact and not processed, come filled with abundant iron, phosphorus, magnesium, manganese, copper, and selenium. The large supply of zinc is a boost for your immune system. The combination of selenium and vitamin E help prevent breast and other cancers. The chromium is highly effective in preventing diabetes. Knowing the true value of a wheat berry is exceptional since most diabetics are forbidden from eating bread products. The fiber will cleanse and feed the microbiome for better brain intellect.

The high magnesium found in the wheat berry protects the heart, prevents muscle cramps, and lessens PMS. That fact should enliven praises from husbands and wives.

The B vitamins in the wheat berry help prevent depression, anxiety, and stress. This factor erases the need for sanitariums. We can enjoy our minds and be ready to praise the Lord and mentally function well every year of life.

God supplied the necessary elements for everyone to be healthy and blessed.

SERVE SOME WHEAT

Our Yeshua, the Hebrew name for Jesus, compares himself to the bread of life. He is our sustainer. He is our Jehovah Rapha healer. Wheat berries freshly ground and baked into homemade bread bring nourishment and delight to our cells. Our cells are sustained for active daily living.

I have included wheat recipes in Part 3 of this book for you to enjoy. Wheat is synonymous in Scripture for other grains such as Emmer, Einkorn, Spelt, Kamut, Hard Red Wheat, Hard White Wheat, and more. To learn more about wheat please check out the *Treasures of Health Nutrition Manual*. When you are ready for the best breads ever—daily or holidays—then the *Satisfied - Baking With Whole Grains* is the perfect cookbook.

WHEAT

GRAINS OF BLESSINGS FROM WHEAT

- Chromium - prevents and controls diabetes

- Fiber - prevents digestive disorder

- Vitamin E and Selenium - prevents breast cancer

- Magnesium – prevents muscle cramps, improves heart function and enhances better memory

- B Vitamins – prevent or reduce anxiety, depression

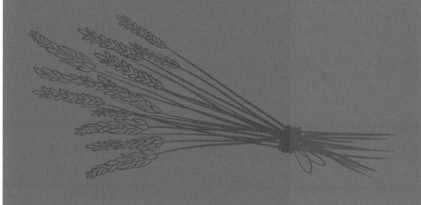

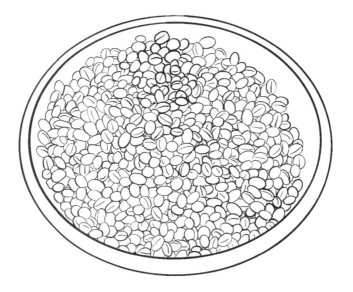

BARLEY

"When he has leveled its surface, does he not then scatter black cumin and sow cumin? He plants wheat in rows and barley in plots, with spelt as their border" (Isaiah 28:25 CSB).

"However, there were ten men among them who said to Ishmael, 'Don't kill us, for we have hidden treasure in the field—wheat, barley, oil, and honey!' So he stopped and did not kill them along with their companions" (Jeremiah 41:8 HCSB).

"There's a boy here who has five barley loaves and two fish—but what are they for so many?" (John 6:9 CSB).

"So they collected them and filled 12 baskets with the pieces from the five barley loaves that were left over by those who had eaten" (John 6:13 CSB).

This fascinating grain is among the earliest known and most nourishing grains ever to be cultivated. Barley is a wonderful gift. It is second to wheat in its status in biblical days (2 Kings 7:1; Revelation 6:6), yet it doesn't take second in nutrition for us.

If you get the opportunity to visit Bethlehem in Israel, you will quickly notice the dry heat and what seems like barren land. Yet, barley can be grown in this area very well. It is a seed that can be cast by hand instead of tilled. It can be harvested by hand as we learn in the account of Ruth harvesting the fields of Boaz. These factors made it easy to grow in small plots by most families. When it is ready for harvest, the barley is stood up in stalks and eventually taken to the threshing floor. In John 4:35 Jesus noted the fields are white for harvest. Those living in the land will say the mature barley fields are white when ready to be harvested.

BARLEY IN THE BIBLE

Barley cannot be missed in numerous biblical accounts throughout Scripture. In fact, it is mentioned more than 35 times. The Feast of Unleavened Bread was an ancient barley harvest festival following the celebration of Passover. Many accounts use barley as the backdrop to the timing of the year or season. Barley matures before wheat (Exodus 9:32) which corresponds with the Jewish calendar month Abib. In Leviticus 23:1 the Israelite is instructed, "Bring to the priest a sheaf of the first grain you harvest." This is a barley sheaf. The grain is mentioned in Exodus, Leviticus, Numbers, Deuteronomy, and Ruth.

During a drought a man brought Elisha the first fruits of barley. This occurred about the same time Elisha overcame death by the pot of stew. And we read that Gideon and his army were called "a loaf of barley bread" in Judges 7:13.

SEEDS OF SPIRITUAL APPLICATION

While wheat adds flavor to the account of Jesus our Yeshua Messiah, the significance of barley heralds the story of wheat. Barley is the backdrop in the love story of Ruth and Boaz. From God delivering on His promises of provisions and grace, Ruth becomes the great-grandmother of King David. Imagine coming from a country that is hostile to the Jews and thn being chosen to be the great grandmother to their king! The account of Ruth (and Naomi) shows that even in the direst circumstances, God is present and blesses humility and obedience. God knows how he is going to fulfill His promises while he provides grace to all who come to him.

He provides more abundantly and exceedingly beyond all we could hope, think, or imagine.

I encourage you to read the complete account of Ruth and Boaz in this treasured book of the Bible. As you read, make note each time barley is mentioned.

The next biblical account is the sharing of five barley loaves and two fish. This is another situation where God provided by feeding thousands with 12 baskets left over. Read this story to the family from John 6. The twelve baskets left over symbolized provisions for the twelve tribes of Israel. Scripture continually brings us back to the account of God delivering His own and fulfilling His promises.

When you serve barley to the family, share these biblical accounts from the old and new testaments to start the conversation of how God always provides. These show a complete portrayal of God's promises, provisions, and grace.

GRAINS WITH PHYSICAL BENEFITS

Barley may be tiny, but it delivers powerful nutrition. Gladiators consumed barley for stamina and strength. Barley prevents inflammation and builds a protective barrier in our digestive lining. While building a digestive defense, it helps our bodies make short chained fatty acids which then improve mental cognition. How many people young and old could use a little more mental clarity?

Barley is our own national guard against invaders in the body and more specifically in the brain—all in one tiny seed. We should create a new action figure named Barley the Brain Builder!

Barley contains an antioxidant to prevent heart disease and lignan oil which prevents the formation of blood clots. The insoluble fiber in barley helps lower LDL cholesterol and block cancer formation by suppressing carcinogens. God-created foods should never surprise us, but that one fact tickles my fancy.

Barley aids in digestion, builds healthy hair and skin and helps the body rid itself of kidney stones. This list of health benefits makes me wonder why barley is not touted as the greatest super food. It compares with the superfood kale, but tastes much better.

SERVE SOME BARLEY

Barley is mostly ignored by foodies, yet it is perfect in the Mediterranean dish tabbouleh. It is also a great addition to soups and salads. You can even enjoy barley grits from Bob's Red Mill topped with fresh apple slices and cinnamon. The rich nutrient list in barley includes B vitamins, iron, calcium, magnesium, manganese, selenium, zinc, copper, protein, amino acids, dietary fiber, beta-glucans, and numerous antioxidants. Barley water (see recipe in Part 3) is very useful for soothing urinary tract or kidney infections. Barley water helps flush out all the toxins from your body, boosts immunity, and improves overall health. Barley water is the perfect heart elixir.

A common question I get is how to cook healthy on a budget? Barley is the healthiest way to stretch any meal and know your family will be satisfied and content. God's foods bring satiety.

> *And the Levite, because he has no portion or inheritance among you, and the alien, the orphan and the widow who are in your town, **shall come and eat and be satisfied**, in order that the Lord your God may bless you in all the work of your hand which you do. (Deuteronomy 14:29 NASB1995 emphasis mine).*

In Part 3 of this book, I have included several recipes, including the healthy drink Barley Water to help you discover new variations of serving barley.

Remember, every meal is an opportunity to share God's promises, provisions, and grace. What we eat connects our mind and memories with what we are hearing and experiencing. Food evokes memories.

When they are grown, children or grandchildren will enjoy barley and immediately their mind will go to the biblical accounts of Ruth and Boaz or Jesus multiplying and serving. Every meal is an opportunity to share and create memories.

And these words which I am commanding you today, shall be on your heart; and you shall **teach them diligently to your children** *and shall talk of them when you sit in your house and when you walk by the way and when you lie down and when you rise up.* (Deuteronomy 6:6-7 NKJV).

BARLEY

GRAINS OF BLESSINGS FROM BARLEY

- Tocotrienol – highest form in barley to prevent heart disease

- Beta-glucans – reduces cancer risk and brings faster recovery

- Lignans – prevents blood clots

- Zinc – improves Immunity

- Vitamin E – for beautiful hair, skin and nails

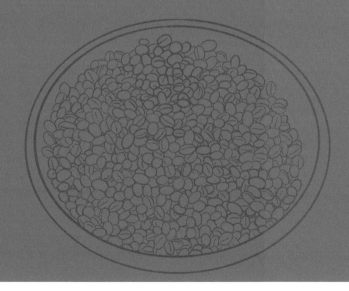

GRAPES

"I found Israel like the grapes in the wilderness" (Hosea 9:10 NASB1995).

"And wine, which makes a human heart cheerful, So that he makes his face gleam with oil, And food, which sustains a human heart" (Psalm 104:15 NASB).

Grapes are mentioned more than 50 times in Scripture. As you walk through the land of Israel today, there are ancient wine presses in many archeological sites including the Garden Tomb area. These unearthed discoveries make it simple to see how the people in earlier times crushed the grapes with their feet while dancing with enthusiasm at the harvest.

"How is the land, is it fat or lean? Are there trees in it or not? Make an effort then to get some of the fruit of the land. Now the time was the time of the first ripe grapes" (Numbers 13:20 NASB1995).

The spies were sent into the Promised Land to learn the condition of the land. Since the number of people entering this promise was immense, the need for food was a daily reminder how much they needed provisions. If a land has fruit, it represents blessings. God's blessings. Notice also the timing of the spies. They were to go to the land for 40 days and bring back the fruit of the land. They were being sent at the time of the grape harvest. This would coincide with the Feast of the Harvest.

"Also you shall observe the Feast of Harvest of the first fruits of your labors from what you sow in the field; also the Feast of the Ingathering at the end of the year when you gather in the fruit of your labors from the field"(Exodus 23:16 NASB).

The Feast of Harvest is also known as the Ingathering or Feast of Tabernacles. This is a significant reminder of God's promises, provisions, and grace. Egypt represents the world and the Promised Land represents rest and peace. The Feast of Tabernacles or Harvest is a time when the work is completed, and we can come into His presence and rest. Complete rest. Not rest as in dying and going to heaven but rest in the peace of God. This is the ultimate gift of grace. The fact that the Israelite spies were going in at such a time meant God had not only heard their cries, he rescued them and prepared a banquet—and was preparing for them to come to rest. The days of hardship were over. The days of wandering in the desert were over. The grapes are the significant food display of promises, provisions, and grace. The Ingathering was right in front of them.

This gathering of fruit was more than just provisions, it was promised. In Numbers 13:2, God promised, "Send out for yourself men so that they may spy out the land of Canaan, which I am going to give to the sons of Israel" (NASB1995). This verse shows the grapes, and the land were promised by God. There was nothing to fear.

The Feast of Tabernacles is the third and final annual requirement for the Jewish males to come to the temple. The Exodus journey started at the inauguration of Passover, which demonstrated God's peace—delivering his promises. The following feast is Shavuot, or most often referred to as Pentecost. Shavuot represents God's power through the giving of the Ten Commandments and later the Holy Spirit.

Now the Feast of Tabernacles is in the peak season of the harvest and signifies a time of rest. After wandering the wilderness for a short time and still overcoming the long exile in Egypt, God delivered them into the Promised Land at the time of the Ingathering, the time of the harvest. Imagine the grapes are ripe, waiting for their arrival. The banquet is set, and the food is being prepared.

Every food promised in this new land was indicative of God's promises. As you remember the story, the spies carried back such large clusters of grapes it required two men with a long pole between them.

Yet, they were afraid. God's provisions and grace were set before them and they cowered. They were sent to discover if the land was fruitful but returned with seeds of fear.

Food was the answer to the quest, yet the spies let obstacles inhibit their view of how much God was providing. This lack of focus on the answer leads them to a 40-year wandering. Losing sight of God's purpose in our lives can do the same today. How we see God at work gives us confidence, but failing to see him at work can invoke fear. This fear transfers to those around us. The Israelite families waiting anxiously saw the return of the men with giant grapes, along with pomegranates and figs and then trembled in fear when they heard the report of giants in the land.

God provided, and the men brought back proof of this blessing, yet they let fear steal the blessing. The banquet would have to wait. The food would go to the enemy. Grace will come to the next generation.

GRAPES ARE A BLESSING OR NOT?

Thus says the LORD: "As the new wine is found in the cluster, And one says, Do not destroy it, for a blessing is in it, So will I do for My servants' sake, That I may not destroy them all" (Isaiah 65:8).[2]

And each of them will sit under his vine and under his fig tree, with no one to make them afraid, for the mouth of the LORD of hosts has spoken (Micah 4:4 NASB1995).

The blessing is as much offered by God as it is taken away by God.

"I will surely snatch them away," declares the Lord; 'There will be no grapes on the vine And no figs on the fig tree, And the leaf will wither; And what I have given them will pass away' (Jeremiah 8:13 NASB1995).

The blessing is taken away when the people are disobedient and irreverent.

Woe is me! For I am Like the fruit pickers, like the grape gatherers. There is not a cluster of grapes to eat, Or a first-ripe fig which I crave (Micah 7:1 NASB1995).

The Lord has sworn by His right hand and by His strong arm, "I will never again give your grain as food for your enemies; Nor will foreigners drink your new wine for which you have labored." But those who garner it will eat it and praise the Lord; And those who gather it will drink it in the courts of My sanctuary (Isaiah 62:8-9 NASB1995).

The verses in Micah show the lack of grapes when people are wicked. Then Isaiah shows God's grace and redemption as the drink of new wine is given back to those who will drink in the courts of God's sanctuary. God will always keep his promises to those who worship him alone. The grapes and wine are continual examples of this throughout Scripture.

WINE AND GRAIN, A BIBLICAL DUO

We learned the biblical value of grain in the reading of wheat and barley. Now we can combine grain and wine to see the full culmination. Since the third day of creation, grain and a fruit have been combined. Melchizedek brought out bread and wine in Genesis 14:18. Jacob was blessed by his father Isaac, with a land of plenty: "Now may the God of the dew of heaven, and the fatness of the earth, And an abundance of grain and new wine" (Genesis 27:28 NASB). In Psalm 104:15 David shares the humbleness of trusting God for provisions and the blessings that come from those provisions.

> And wine to gladden the heart of man, oil to make his face shine and bread to strengthen man's heart (Psalm 104:15 ESV).

The tribute offering under the Law required both grain and a quart of wine (Leviticus 23:13). Both bread and wine were found on the Table of Showbread, signifying communion for Israel. Bread and wine signify Jesus Christ at His supper, and by eating them, we remember his sacrifice with new bread and wine ourselves.

> I am the true vine, and My Father is the vinedresser. Every branch in Me that does not bear fruit, He takes away; and every branch that bears fruit, He prunes it so that it may bear more fruit. You are already clean because of the word which I have spoken to you. Abide in Me and I in you. As the branch cannot bear fruit of

itself unless it abides in Me. I am the vine, you are the branches; he who abides in Me and I in him, he bears much fruit, for apart from Me you can do nothing (John 15:1-5 NASB1995).

The significance of these seven foods starts as provisions and a promise and will continue to be a blessing—if—the Israelites focus on the answers God is showing them and not wander into fear of the giants in the land.

GRAPES DURING JESUS DAY

Many of the farmers in the Holy Land, even during the days Jesus walked through Galilee, were subsistence farmers. The purpose of this farm was to provide food for the farmer's family. Most of the farmland in Galilee was owned by subsistence farmers. The average family owned from one half acre up to seven acres. On this family farm, they grew flax for clothing, wheat and barley for bread, grapes for wine and raisins, and olives for oil and brining. Many farmers also had fruit trees. Their food supply surrounded them. God's provision.

PHYSICAL BENEFITS

Grapes are a cluster of nutrition. Grapes come loaded with iron, potassium, phosphorus, magnesium, manganese, and calcium. Grapes contain flavonoids with powerful antioxidants. Grapes have vitamins to nourish every cell in the body.

Current studies prove the juice and skin of the muscadine grape helps in the prevention of the formation of plaque on the arteries and prevents DNA damage. The muscadine grape skin and seeds contain a high content of resveratrol, which can stall the onset of neurodegenerative disease and strengthen the activity of the brain. Resveratrol can also help prevent cancers of the breast, colon, and stomach. Grapes promote stem cell growth, which improves cell viability and improves immunity.

Science Direct, a website which explores the best scientific, technical, and medical research, listed even more benefits from grapes and resveratrol. This list includes anti-obesity, cardio protective, neuroprotective, antitumor, antidiabetic, antioxidants, anti-age effects, and glucose metabolism. And antibacterial effects against food-borne pathogens are also present in grapes.[3]

When we combine preventing DNA damage along with the high vitamins C, A, and B, grapes will help us look younger longer. Now, let's confess, total transparency here, who wants to look younger than our friends?

I need to stop writing here and go grab a bowl of grapes. Studying nutrition biblically makes me crave God's provisions every day. I hope you are sensing it as well.

SERVE SOME GRAPES

Grapes are common in diets today. One fun way to enjoy them is frozen whole for a quick snack. They can also be dipped in yogurt and chopped nuts or chia seeds before freezing them. Doing this trick with grapes and becoming known as the gourmet granny.

Try grapes in fruit cups, fruit salads, and fruit compotes. Grapes combine well with avocado, grapefruits sections, melon balls, or strawberries.

GRAPES AS HONEY

In the Bible and other ancient literature, the word honey could also refer to fruit juices boiled into syrup and used to flavor foods. Juice from grapes, pomegranates, dates, and figs were used in this way. In Part 3 there is a recipe for Pomegranate Molasses. This is a fruit honey. Grapes or grape juice could be used in this recipe in place of pomegranates.

See Part 3 for some unique grape recipes.

GRAPES

FRUITS OF BLESSINGS FROM GRAPES

- Vitamin C – protects from DNA damage

- Tannins – strengthens capillaries to protect the heart and circulatory system

- Quercetin – Minimizes inflammation

- Quick Energy – the perfect energizing snack before, during or after a workout

- Ellagic acid, resveratrol – perfect cancer prevention food

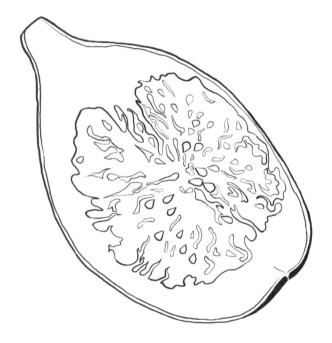

FIGS

The fig tree has ripened its figs, And the vines in blossom have given forth their fragrance. Arise, my darling, my beautiful one, and come along (Song of Solomon 2:13 NASB1995).

He who tends the fig tree will eat its fruit; And he who cares for his master will be honored (Proverbs 27:18 NASB1995).

Figs are best when tended daily. When the ripe fruit is left too long on the tree, the fragrance will attract pests. Proverbs says the person who tends the tree well will enjoy its fruit. The same is true for us. When we tend our relationship with God daily and seek his promises and grace, his provisions are ripe in season.

FIGS IN THE BIBLE

Figs are mentioned in the Bible more than 40 times. We don't venture far into the pages of Scripture before we discover the first mention of figs. Genesis 3:7 takes us to the garden room of Adam and Eve as they sew fig leaves together to make themselves loin coverings. They needed covering since they were now in the know about good and evil.

Figs are mentioned again in the days of the Exodus. The Israelites were an interesting group of people. They were delivered from being held captive, set free to cross the Red Sea, saw God do the most amazing miracles, but they still complained about the lack of figs.

And why have you made us come up from Egypt, to bring us in to this wretched place? It is not a place of grain or figs or vines or pomegranates, nor is there water to drink (Numbers 20:5 NASB1995).

Throughout Scripture, figs or the fig tree is a barometer of the health or status of the nation of Israel. Figs are compared to blessings. Just as the rich flavor and sweetness of the fig bless the taste buds and body, the tree represents the sweet parts of life.

Figs stand as a symbol of prosperity, well-being, and security.

During the time of Moses, the fig tree was one of the foods the Lord used to describe the blessings of the Promised Land.

It is a land of wheat and barley; of grapevines, fig trees, and pomegranates; of olive oil and honey (Deuteronomy 8:8 NLT).

Blessings, as we learned in grapes, are most often tied to obedience to God. The Israelites required refining from the corruption they had learned from the Egyptians and needed to worship God before they could truly experience His blessings. The theme of figs serves as a symbol for blessing throughout the Old Testament. And contrarily, figs are a symbol of warning, destruction, and failure.

> *Now in the morning, when He was returning to the city, He became hungry, Seeing a lone fig tree by the road, He came to it and found nothing on it except leaves only; and He said to it, 'No longer shall there ever be any fruit from you.' And at once the fig tree withered* (Matthew 21:18-19 NASB1995).

In this verse in Matthew, we see the example of the warning I just mentioned. This verse is questioned and explained by many theologians. The question is, 'Why would Jesus curse a fig tree that is not in season?' As I have seen in my own yard, when fig trees have leaves they have small fruit hiding under the leaves. The fruit is so small a person passing by might not see them. Yet, they show the health of the tree and the promises of sweet fruit to come.

The town of Bethany where Jesus was venturing was literally the 'house of figs". It was not yet the season for the harvest of figs (Mark 11:13). But there was such a thing as early figs (see Isaiah 28:4, Jeremiah 24:2, Hosea 9:10, and Nahum 3:12). Fig fruit would appear first, then the leaves. So when Jesus saw leaves, he expected to find some early figs.

Yet, why did Jesus curse the tree?

Matthew Henry shares the answer this way:

> Christ went to the tree expecting fruit, but finding none, he sentenced it to a perpetual barrenness. This cursing on the barren fig-tree, represents the state of hypocrites in general; and teaches us,

> 1. That the fruit of fig trees may justly be expected from those that have the leaves. Christ looks for the power of religion from those that make profession of it.

2. Christ's just expectations from flourishing
   professors are often frustrated and disappointed.
   Many have a name to live and are not alive indeed.

3. The sin of barrenness is justly punished with the
   curse and plague of barrenness; let no fruit grow on
   thee forever.

As one of the chief blessings, which was the first, is *Be fruitful,* so one of the saddest curses is, *Be no more fruitful.* Hypocrites may look plausible for a time, but their profession will soon come to nothing.

God knows the heart of man. The fig tree looked great with a bounty of leaves, yet it was barren in its fruit. We too, may look good to others but our heart must be bearing fruit.

This lesson escapes the Twelve, who are more amazed at the speed with which Jesus' words come true (Matthew 21:20). Christ does not focus on hypocrisy yet (vv. 28–32). Instead, he teaches on prayer, informing His followers that believing prayer can accomplish great things (vv. 21–22).

Scriptural Examples:

So Judah and Israel lived securely, everyone under his vine and his fig tree, from Dan even to Beersheba, all the days of Solomon (1 Kings 4:25 NASB).

And all the heavenly lights will wear away, And the sky will be rolled up like a scroll; All its lights will also wither away As a leaf withers from the vine, Or as one withers from the fig tree (Isaiah 34:4 NASB).

*Woe to me! For I am like harvests of summer fruit, like gleanings of grapes. There is not a cluster of grapes **left** to eat, **Nor** an early fig, **which** I crave* (Micah 7:1 NASB emphasis mine).

PHYSICAL BENEFITS

Nutritionally figs nourish and satisfy your cells. The fiber content in figs balances blood sugars and promotes satiety. Figs are the perfect diabetes preventer.

This delicious fruit is loaded with calcium to build strong bones in children and sustains bone density in adults. Figs have potassium to control blood pressure and iron to prevent anemia in pregnancy.

Figs contain the vitamins C, B1, B2, B3, B6, folate (B9), A, E, and K to give you a complete menu of nutrients to prevent memory loss and reduce stress levels when your mind is overwhelmed.

Details such as these make me wish I could go back 20 or 30 years and add figs into my diet.

When these nutrients are all-in-one as in the eating of one fig, the exponential benefit to the body includes stimulating blood circulation, cleansing the blood, and adding color to the skin.

1 Samuel 30:11 tells us about an Egyptian who was found in the field and brought to King David. He was given fig cake and clusters of raisins to revive his spirit after 3 days of sickness.

Hezekiah tells of another healing from the use of figs.

In those days Hezekiah became mortally ill. And Isaiah the prophet, the son of Amoz, came to him and said to him, "'Thus says the LORD: Set your house in order, for you shall die and not live." Then Hezekiah turned his face to the wall, and prayed to the LORD, and said, "Remember now, O LORD, I beseech Thee, how I have walked before Thee in truth and with a whole heart, and have done what is good in Thy sight." And Hezekiah wept bitterly (Isaiah 38:1,2,3 NASB 1995).

The Lord answered Hezekiah's prayer and sent His prophet Isaiah with the following message, "Let them take a lump of figs, and apply it as a poultice on the boil, and he shall recover" (2 Kings 20:7).

Figs are used throughout the Bible for a reminder of God's promises

- how he cares for Israel

- how he desires to satisfy the needs of his own

- how he heals the land.

SERVE FIGS

Figs have been a topic many times on our blog, YouTube videos, and recipes. In my yard, I have a fig tree, which produces buckets of figs. I have a collection of recipes and keep them out on my counter. Some of the recipes I serve include fresh figs, apple fig crumble, and even blueberry fig jam. There is no end to the possibilities of using figs in the kitchen. I hope you enjoy the recipes added to this book in Part 3.

FIGS

FRUITS OF BLESSINGS FROM FIGS

- Perfect food for satiety

- Calcium – great for athletes

- B Complex – prevent memory loss

- Iron – prevent anemia, especially in pregnancy

- Fiber – no more constipation food

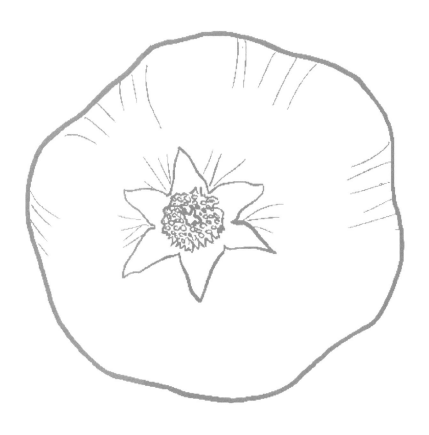

POMEGRANATES

Your temples are like a slice of a pomegranate behind your veil (Song of Solomon 4:3).

On my first trip to Israel, every sight was a learning experience, and every location had a gift shop. A lot can be learned about the land of Israel from the gift shop. *Or so I told my husband.* The image of the pomegranate fruit adorned everything from Kiddush cups and candle sticks to Torah covers and crowns. I knew pomegranates were in the Bible but when I returned home, I did a deep dive into the research of pomegranates. I learned the true significance of pomegranates in biblical days.

Pomegranates in the Bible

Pomegranates are the least of the seven foods of the Promised Land mentioned in the Bible, yet that does not mean they are insignificant. Quite the contrary, pomegranates always represent blessings and royalty.

Is the seed still in the barn? Even including the vine, the fig tree, the pomegranate and the olive tree, it has not borne fruit. Yet from this day on I will bless you (Haggai 2:19 NASB 1995).

The pomegranate appears as a symbol of love in the Song of Solomon.

Your branches are an orchard of pomegranates With delicious fruits, henna with nard plants (Song of Solomon 4:13 NASB).

Your temples are like a slice of a pomegranate, Behind your veil (Song of Solomon 6:7 NASB).

They adorned the hem of the High Priest's robe by stitching images of pomegranates woven from sky-blue, purple, and scarlet yarn interspersed with gold bells. We know that the color blue in God's pattern represents the heavens, purple is for royalty, and red (scarlet) for blood—for life. Perhaps the pomegranates were to be a reminder of God's mercy and covenant with his people, and his plan of redemption.

On its hem you shall make pomegranates of blue and purple and scarlet yarns, around its hem, with bells of gold between them, a golden bell and a pomegranate, a golden bell and a pomegranate, around the hem of the robe. And it shall be on Aaron when he ministers, and its sound shall be heard when he goes into the Holy Place before the LORD, and when he comes out, so that he does not die (Exodus 28:33-35 ESV).

King Solomon decorated the columns of the first temple with more than 400 engraved pomegranates. Rows and rows of pomegranates crowned the temple and pillars, declaring God's goodness and blessing to his covenant people.

These were the same pillars carted off to Babylon with the fall of Jerusalem and the enslavement of Judah.

Now a capital of bronze was on it; and the height of each capital was five cubits, with network and pomegranates upon the capital all around, all of bronze. And the second pillar was like these, including pomegranates. There were ninety-six exposed pomegranates; all the pomegranates numbered a hundred on the network all around (Jeremiah 52:22-23 LSB).

Pomegranates are a food of sweet memory to the Israelites. They enjoyed these fruits in the land of Egypt. We know this because of their complaining.

Why have you made us come up from Egypt, to bring us in to this wretched place? It is not a place of grain or figs or vines or pomegranates, nor is there water to drink (Numbers 20:5 NASB 1995).

Now, let's put this complaining into context. This verse is just seven chapters after the Israelite spies returned with large poles carrying a single cluster of grapes between two men along with pomegranates and figs. (Numbers 13:22) They were offered land with the harvest ready and they were afraid. Now they are complaining because as they see it, God was not providing.

Pomegranates were engraved in the ancient coins of Judea. They represented royalty. As we have our presidents on coins, pomegranates were used in Biblical days.

Seeds in pomegranates are called arils. It is believed each pomegranate contains 613 arils. This number corresponds to the number of laws in the Pentateuch.

As an all-out biblical foodie, I had to know if this number was true. So, on the internet *which is always the gospel truth*, I found another foodie who tested the theory. He gathered pomegranates from all over the world and counted the seeds (arils) in each one. Some had more and others had less, so, the theory is not true. But, when he averaged the results, the average number was 613. I cannot prove this story to be true, but it reminds me of the importance of God's laws and how the law directed us to our need for a Savior. And if we share stories like these to our friends and family, we can always come back to that fact, we all need a Savior since we cannot keep the whole law on our own. And when that touches your heart like it does mine, the pomegranate takes on a new flavor of love.

SEEDS OF PHYSICAL BENEFITS

Today the pomegranate delivers not just beauty and artwork for the columns of the Temple but for your beauty as well. Pomegranates have antioxidant properties, which have an anti-aging effect. It is rich in vitamin C, tannins, anthocyanins, and ellagic acid, all of which reverse free radical damage and protect your skin from further damage. This includes the sun.

The flavonols, which are a type of antioxidant, in pomegranates are shown to prevent inflammation in the body and may help relieve symptoms of arthritis. They protect against arthritis and help alleviate rheumatoid arthritis and osteoarthritis.

These same antioxidants are proven to help prevent cancers, especially breast cancer in both men and women. This action comes from the punicic acid in the pomegranate seed oil, which is an omega-5 long chain polyunsaturated fatty acid. This acid has been shown to block breast cancer cell proliferation. The cancer benefit is also good for men.

In a study of male subjects with recurrent prostate cancer and rising prostate-specific antigen (PSA) levels, researchers found that drinking pomegranate juice extract significantly slowed the rate at which PSA was rising.[4]

The polyphenols have been proven to help lower blood pressure and improve heart health. And the seeds in the arils are perfect for removing the buildup of plaque on teeth.

Because of their high antioxidant content, pomegranates are a boost to the immune system. Pomegranate juice has three times the antioxidant power of red wine or green tea.

SERVE POMEGRANATES

Pomegranates serve well as topping on salads, oatmeal, or even added to freshly brewed tea. I love just a cup of arils with nothing else. I think it is the most pleasing delight ever. I have included recipes for you to enjoy the pomegranate in new, delicious ways in Part 3.

POMEGRANATES

SEEDS OF BLESSINGS IN POMEGRANATES

- Antioxidant punicalagins – prevents cancers

- Antioxidants – beautiful and youthful skin

- Anti-carcinogenic – Especially for prostate cancers

- Polyphenols – prevents plaque buildup
  in the heart

- Vitamin C – protects against heart disease, cancer
  and eye problems

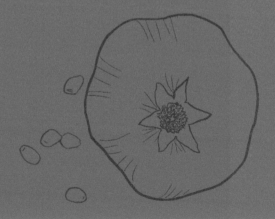

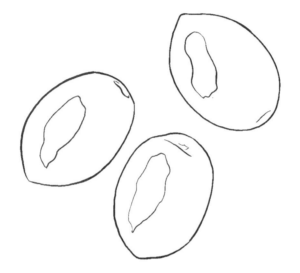

OLIVES

But as for me, I am like a green olive tree in the house of God; I trust in the lovingkindness of God forever and ever (Psalm 52:8 NASB 1995).

On our second trip to Jerusalem, we planted a biblical foods prayer garden. The olive trees were already established and since it was October, they were ready to harvest. We were each given garden rakes, used mostly for grass clippings, and told to start gathering the olives. As we raked the trees the olives fell on the tarp below. It was a memorable experience. Then we gathered all the olives and removed the twigs and leaves to put them in large 5 gallon buckets. From there it was off to the olive press. We did not pull up to a stone mill with two donkeys pulling from opposite sides. We pulled up to what looked like a lawn mower repair shop. Then as we were ushered into the back room we saw the press. The olives were sent up a conveyor belt and then dropped onto the top of the press. As they were crushed through each descending layer of mesh the oil became more refined.

The end result was the most beautiful olive oil I have ever seen. The color was a beautiful olive green and the aroma was a rich roasted-nuts smell.

A trip to Israel typically does not include raking olives and watching the press, but it does include time sitting on the Mount of Olives as you see the Kidron valley below.

OLIVES IN THE BIBLE

So many biblical accounts happen on this very spot. From the OT to the NT to the end of Revelation when Christ returns. Olives, Mount of Olives, and the olive branch bring an in-depth learning of who God is.

Olives offer us in-depth understanding in the Word and God's presence. The first mention of olives is when the dove brings back an olive branch to Noah as a sign of God's promises to care for Noah and his family. (See Genesis 8:11) When the dove returned to Noah on the ark with the olive branch in its beak, it was a sign of God's promises, provisions, and grace. God had a remnant of followers to start the new world after the flood. The olive branch as a symbol of peace was a delicate reminder of that promise.

> *The dove came to him toward evening, and behold, in her beak was a freshly picked olive leaf. So Noah knew that the water was abated from the earth* (Genesis 8:11 NASB 1995).

In Psalm 52:8, written above, we see another glimpse in the Word of the significance of olives. David is sharing how he is plucked up by the roots; but like an olive tree he is planted and rooted, fixed and flourishing. He is established. Mathew Henry in his commentary on this verse shares:

What must we do that we may be as a green olive tree?

1. We must live a life of faith and holy confidence in God and his grace.

2. We must live a life of thankfulness and holy joy in God.[5]

Olives are most known to represent peace. Yet, that peace comes not from being weak and hidden but from being steadfast and courageous. It is a peace of knowing whose you are and believing in that faith. Peace is knowing God always fulfills his promises and provides for his own. And in the example of grace, the olive branch being shared between two people as a symbol of peace is an example of the grace God extends to us. Peace.

Olives are also a symbol of blessing, fruitfulness, and health.

Your wife shall be like a fruitful vine within your house, Your children like olive plants around your table (Psalm 128:3 NASB).

And houses full of all good things which you did not fill, and hewn cisterns which you did not dig, vineyards and olive trees which you did not plant, and you eat and are satisfied (Deuteronomy 6:11 NASB1995).

Is the seed still in the barn? Even including the vine, the fig tree, the pomegranate and the olive tree, it has not borne fruit. Yet from this day on I will bless you (Haggai 2:19 NASB1995).

Our self-proclaimed Jewish Yankee tour guide in Israel gave our group a quiz at the end of our tour. There was only one question. Could we identify the olive tree?

One of my favorite verses to sing is:

For you will go out with joy and be led forth with peace; The mountains and the hills will break forth into shouts of joy before you, and all the trees of the field will clap their hands (Isaiah 55:12 NASB1995).

The leaves of the olive tree have a beautiful silvery underside distinguishing them from the other trees. When they blow in the wind it appears they are clapping. Add to this the view of the Mount of Olives, and you can see in your heart and mind Jesus returning while the olive trees sway and the leaves clap. With that in mind I aced the test!

In biblical days, the olive oil had three main uses:

- the first pressing was for offerings in the temple

- the second pressing was for fire

- the third pressing was for lighting in their homes.

Olive oil was used for anointing kings as a sign they were chosen by God to rule. The Israelites anointed the tabernacle and all its furnishings with olive oil.

For those who have traveled to Israel there is no place as special as the Mount of Olives as a place to pray and weep for all that our Lord has done for us and also to shed tears of happiness for what he is coming to do.

In Deuteronomy 8:8, the description of the Promised Land reads with a pause in the middle.

A land of wheat and barley, of vines and fig trees and pomegranates, a land of olive oil and honey (NASB1995)

The first five foods mentioned—wheat, barley, grapes (vines), figs, and pomegranates—were enjoyed while in Egypt. These foods are mentioned in the way they grow. Wheat and barley are cultivated in the field. Grapes (vines), figs, and pomegranates are grown on trees or vines. Then the verse takes a pause with the word *land*. Following that gap are two foods: olives and honey. These are foods the Israelites had not yet experienced in Egypt or the wilderness. When the Jews complained in the desert, they mentioned figs, grapes, and pomegranates, but not olives and dates. Rabbi Meir Simcha taught this as proof that they didn't have those foods in Egypt. Even today, the land of Israel is distinguished through these two foods.

I will share next about dates and how the best dates in the entire world were grown near the Dead Sea. The same is true of olives. Olives were first discovered in archeology in the land of Israel; from there the next discovery dated later was in Egypt. From there olives made it through the trade route into Greece, Rome, and Spain. In later years the Spanish explorers brought olives to the Americas.

PHYSICAL BENEFITS

Olives are rich in phytonutrients. *Phyto* means plant. These are rich nutrients from the plants God designed for not only the Israelites to be blessed and enjoy but for us too.

Eating olives inhibits the production of chronic inflammation which helps the body heal and remove inflammation.

Olives are the queen of antioxidants and help to lower LDL cholesterol while raising HDL cholesterol, prevent nerve cell damage, and increase the blood levels of glutathione. Glutathione is the master antioxidant in our body. It is a shield for our defense. A defense against pathogens, viruses and cancers.

The phenols in olives protect against cancers, especially of the digestive system such as the colon. Olives also slow down the aging process and prevent bone loss.

Olive oil is also known for its beauty properties. Olive oil reduces wrinkles around eyes when massaged around the eyes every morning and evening. It is also the perfect makeup remover since it does not clog pores.

An olive oil dipping sauce with freshly milled bread in the evening will soften the bowels and help with constipation. The oil boosts metabolism and activates pancreatic enzymes to help with digestion.

Olives and olive oil are rich with vitamins such as C, B, A, E, and K, plus minerals such as calcium, iron, magnesium, phosphorus, potassium, zinc, and selenium. The vitamins A, E and K are fat soluble vitamins. This means they need a fat carrier to reach the cells. Eating olives gives you the fat carrier and the vitamin all riding in the same transport. A diet with these vitamins, for example a store-bought multivitamin, without a healthy oil to carry it into the cells will not enjoy the benefit from these vitamins. Olives deliver a complete alphabet of nutrition.

SERVE OLIVES

I know you already enjoy olive oil in your cooking and dips. Making your own infused oils is a new delight and fun foodie experience. Any herb added to the oil will impart a flavor that will excite your taste buds. Use a clean jar, fill two thirds with oil and then add an herb such as a rosemary twig, or sage. The flavor keeps becoming tastier the longer it sits.

Be creative. Try new recipes, especially the ones I've included in Part 3.

It is almost time to go to the grocery store with all this knowledge of these blessed foods. But before you go, let's finish your list with the last food: dates/honey.

OLIVES

FRUITS OF BLESSING IN OLIVES

- Nutrient: squalene – heart protecting and relieves inflammation

- Oleic acid –calm and soothe the skin, and boost the ability to remove unwanted fat cells.

- Vitamin E – keep skin wrinkle free and hair glossy

- Vitamin E – reduces hot flashes and helps expel gallstones

DATES

The righteous man will flourish like the palm tree, he will grow like a cedar in Lebanon (Psalm 92:12 NASB1995).

And she used to sit under the palm tree of Deborah between Ramah and Bethel in the hill country of Ephraim; and the sons of Israel came up to her for judgment (Judges 4:5 NASB1995).

And He said, "If you will give earnest heed to the voice of the LORD your God and do what is right in His sight, and give ear to His commandments, and keep all His statutes, I will put none of the diseases on you which I have put on the Egyptians; for I the Lord am your healer." Then they came to Elim where there were twelve springs of water and seventy date palms, and then camped there beside the waters (Exodus 15:26-27 NASB1995).

The word *honey* appears in Scripture 55 times. What most Christians don't realize is this word honey actually refers to date or fig honey. Except in two references: Judges 14:8-9, when Samson took honey from the lion's carcass, and 1 Samuel 14:27 when Jonathan dipped his rod in a honeycomb during a battle and his countenance brightened. There is one other reference to bee honey as Jacob sends honey to Egypt as a gift to the king, Genesis 43:11. During the famine only wild foods were found. Wild flowers and bees can live during times of famine. The springs are dry and the fruit of date palms wither. This brings the agreed conclusion the word honey in Deuteronomy 8, is honey made from dates.

DATES IN THE BIBLE

In fact, the oldest writings in the Jerusalem Talmud, Bikkurim, Chapter 1, Mishna 3 states the honey referenced in Deuteronomy 8 is from dates. The Hebrews regarded dates as a symbol of righteousness, being honorable, and being beautiful.

The Israelites were promised a land flowing with milk and honey in Exodus 3:8. This honey is the Hebrew word *dvash* and it is predominately a thick syrup made from dates. In the recipes of this book, I have included a very sweet date paste for you to experiment with in various recipes. The biblical reference to honey in Deuteronomy 8 is referencing dates. As you learn the fascinating nature of dates, you will see why dates are on the 7 foods promised list.

There are few mentions of dates in Scripture, yet we can learn about dates from writers such as Josephus and rabbinical writings like the Mishnah. These writers teach us dates were a favored food as early as 4,500 years before the birth of Jesus, our Yeshua Messiah. Date palms grew along the southern Jordan River and were cultivated around Jericho. In fact, Jericho was known as the city of date palm trees. Herod the Great owned extensive date palm orchards.[7] Many historians believe these orchards flourished because of the salinity of the soil and the natural springs in the area. This leads to the most delicious sweet fruit to be enjoyed at harvest but also for months to come.

Dates, as referenced as palm trees, were a prominent fruit as mentioned in Joel 1:11-12.

> *Be ashamed, you farmers, Wail, you vinedressers, For the wheat and the barley; Because the harvest of the field has perished.*
>
> *The vine has dried up, the fig tree is withered; the pomegranate tree, the palm tree also, all the trees of the field are withered; surely the joy has withered away from the sons of men (NKJV).*

Dates from the palm tree share in the reference with the promised fruits of the land.

Dates grown in Beit' Shean, Jordan Valley, Jericho, and the Dead Sea regions were praised all throughout Greece and Rome as the finest in the region. These dates were sweet and juicy and yet, they were able to be preserved for months. Dates grown in other areas were a dry date that was good to eat when harvested but would soon rot if left unattended. The dry dates grown in Babylon were commonly used as fodder for animals.

Josephus (37-85 A.D.) gives biblical references and precedents for the importance of the date in Israelite history, and describes the dates of Jericho and the Dead Sea: "Here (in Jericho) is the richest region of Judaea in which are grown many date palms of excellent quality."[7]

Dates are and were the perfect traveler's food. They were enjoyed fresh, dried, and even baked into cakes. As in the story of the celebration of bringing the ark to Jerusalem, David gave gifts of food to each Israelite man and woman. He gave a loaf of bread, a piece of meat and a cake of raisins. Raisins referred not only to dried grapes but any dried fruit. The term raisins mean dried fruit. Remember David spent many of his young years in the Ein Gedi region, which is considered the land of palms near the Dead Sea. David would know the best raisin cake restaurant around for miles. Dates were found on the palms trees over the entire region of Israel in biblical days and even today. (See 2 Samuel 6:19 and 1 Chronicles 16:3.)

We can read this in Song of Solomon 7:7, "This stature of yours is like a palm tree."

> *They are upright, like a palm tree, and they cannot speak; They must be carried, Because they cannot go by themselves." Israelites patterned their gods after the provisions God blessed them with* (Jeremiah 10:5 NKJV).

> *Then he carved all the walls of the temple all around, both the inner and outer sanctuaries, with carved figures of cherubim, palm trees and open flowers* (1 Kings 6:29, 32 NKJV).

> *And also the Amorites who dwelt in Hazezon Tamar* (Genesis 14:7). *"*

Tamar means land of dates. Hazezon Tamar noted in this Genesis verse is later referred to as Ein Gedi in 2 Chronicles 20:2. The name Tamar given to women was taken from the date palm. The name Tamar means gracious and upright form

Dates – Promises, Provisions, and Grace

The Israelites journeyed to Elim and were greeted by twelve wells of waters and seventy date palm trees. This was a visual reminder of God's promises, provisions, and grace. The dates and water were waiting for their arrival. This is a snapshot of what is to come when they reach the final destination of the Promised Land. Yet, not long after this, they journeyed on again only to fall into the habits of tradition to complain of all they left in Egypt, of the pots of meat and bread to the full. God did not cast them away for their complaining, he delivered grace in the form of manna and quail. Food again becomes the reminder of all God can and will do when we seek him.

FRUIT OF PHYSICAL BENEFITS

It is a delight to enjoy dates today. If you or your family have been feeding on processed foods such as Pop Tarts™, then the sweet sticky flavor of dates may not be an instant gratification. Yet, the nutrition in dates should make this a daily delight.

The Babylonian Talmud suggests eating dates: "They are good in the morning and in the evening. They are bad in the afternoon, but there is nothing like it to dispel moodiness, stomach-aches, and hemorrhoids." This ancient writing sums it up. Dates benefit the body by helping with mental clarity, and all through the digestive tract.

The high fiber content in dates is linked to lower rates of certain cancers especially pancreatic and abdominal cancers. As fiber helps remove toxic waste from the digestive system it is also food to the good bacteria in the microbiome. Fiber is a prebiotic. The bacteria feed on this fiber and say *thank you* by delivering B vitamins, which is why it is recommended for moodiness. B vitamins, which I mentioned with the other foods improve your happiness. The B vitamins come from the bacteria and also from the fruit. They help prevent depression and release energy. B vitamins are essential to your happiness and health. I am sure we can all make a list of people we need to serve dates to for dinner.

Because of their nutritious load of vitamins and minerals, dates are the perfect food for muscle strength, correcting stomach disorders, balancing the nervous system, and protecting the heart as it lowers LDL cholesterol and has a positive effect on weak hearts.

Dates are the perfect food for everyone. They are loaded with nutrients including potassium, vitamin C, seven of the eight B vitamins, minerals such as calcium, magnesium, phosphorus, zinc copper, and essential oils, plus beta carotene.

When we feed children dates in place of overly sweetened processed foods, they will be able to process math better, read and retain the information, plus have fewer sick days. The struggle will be changing the diet from over-processed foods to dates. But when you succeed, health benefits will multiply. The short transition time of changing the diet will serve extras for years with greater health.

DATES – SUMMARY

It is a sweet way to read the Bible when we see God's provisions still available to us today. Serving dates to our family is a daily or weekly way to be a reminder of the biblical accounts to share. My favorite is when David is hiding in the caves of Ein Gedi and snips off the corner of Saul's robe (See 1 Samuel 24-31).

These caves in Ein Gedi are perfect for hiking on your next visit to Israel. You will be able to swim in the basin of the waterfalls while casting a view of the beautiful Dead Sea. As you see the plains of the Jordan Valley remember the vision Ezekiel wrote about, which will happen in days of Revelation. The sea will be teaming with fish and the entire region will be the new garden. Ezekiel wrote:

> He said to me: "This water flows towards the eastern region and goes down into the Arabah (the Jordan Valley), where it enters the Sea (the Dead Sea). When it empties into the Sea, the salty water becomes fresh. Swarms of living creatures will live wherever the river flows. There will be large numbers of fish, because this water flows there and makes the salt water fresh; so where the river flows everything will live. Fishermen will stand along the shore; from Ein Gedi to En Eglaim there will be places for spreading nets. The fish will be of many kinds, like the fish of the Great Sea (the Mediterranean) (Ezekiel 47:8-10 NIV).

God's Word comes alive as we taste and see why he uses food to not only nourish us but to satisfy our cravings. Each of these reminders of God's promises can be shared while enjoying a serving of my Baked Fruit Delight topped with Strawberry Sauce.

Enjoy the date recipes while you serve your family a rich biblical heritage.

DATES

Fruits of Blessings in Dates

- Fiber – Prevents Diabetes

- B Vitamins – No More Moodiness

- Flavonoids – reduce risk of Alzheimer's and cancer

- Calcium, phosphorus, and magnesium – strong bones

- Antioxidants – brain boosters and less anxiety

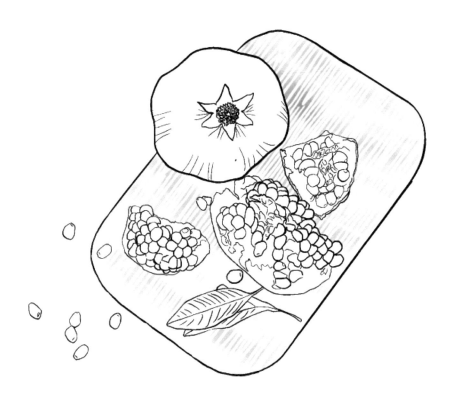

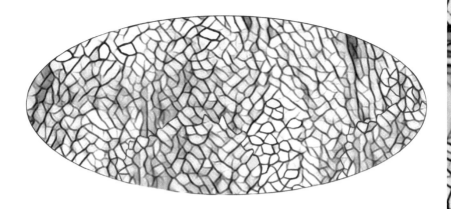

7 FLAVORS OF GRACE

Earlier we read the passage in Deuteronomy 8:8, which said they would "lack nothing."

Every system in the body—every cell—is nourished and protected when we eat these seven foods. When the known nutrients are calculated from these seven foods, there is no missing element for not only sustaining life but to live life abundantly as the Word teaches. (See John 10:10). God provides for our physical health in these foods.

When the cells take in whole foods such as the seven we have covered, they automatically respond with increased energy and clarity of mind. The ability to function at high performance becomes the new normal.

In fact, our cells recognize God's goodness even before we can say, "Thank you, God."

The Israelites didn't have the electron microscopes or imaging methods used today in food science. They had no way of knowing the flavors of His grace would benefit the cellular structure in such a fulfilling way. God wanted them to trust him. Not go elsewhere for their deliverance nor their delight.

No other foods, altered and imitation foods such as we have today, can deliver the nutritive blessings as these foods God designed for us from the beginning.

He prepared the Israelites hearts, minds, and taste buds to experience His grace as they followed his commandments. The flavor of grace satisfies and will always satisfy.

This is true for us. He wants us to be satisfied in him and His commandments and therefore delight in His grace. His grace includes enjoyable foods.

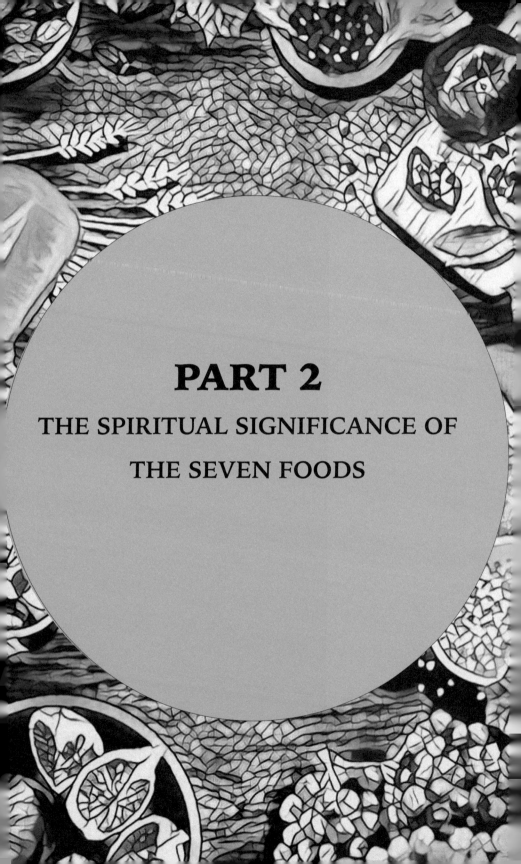

PART 2

THE SPIRITUAL SIGNIFICANCE OF

THE SEVEN FOODS

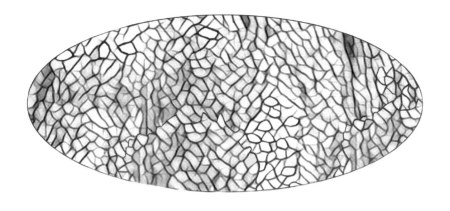

A BUFFET OF GOD'S GRACE

In October 2016, we took our second trip to Israel—a mission trip. We came prepared to plant these seven biblical foods in the center of Jerusalem, just down the street from the Garden of Gethsemane, nestled in a prayer garden. This garden is surrounded by various ethnic groups on every side. Every day people walk along the sidewalk and look through the open bars of the fence into the prayer garden and read the scriptures on the walls and see the food being grown as a reminder of God's promises, provisions, and grace.

Yet, before we could make this trip, I needed to thoroughly understand why God chose these specific foods. Why didn't he choose yogurt, cheese, apples, and pears? Through numerous phone calls, emails, and conversations with universities in the US and in Israel and dozens of books and commentaries, I found the answers.

Within the seven foods—wheat, barley, grapes, pomegranates, figs, olives, and dates—there is a menu, a buffet of God's grace.

The common denominator for these seven foods is the celebration of our Lord in the Feast of our Lord. And it starts with the calendar of days between Passover and Shavuot: Pentecost. Fifty days when the Canaanites worshiped their multiple gods fervently, and the same 50 days when God told the Israelites to focus on him.

Beware lest you forget the Lord your God by not keeping His commandments and His ordinances and His statues which I am commanding you today.

Lest, when you have eaten and are satisfied, and have built good houses and lived in them, then your heart becomes proud and you forget the Lord your God who brought you out from the land of Egypt, out of the house of slavery (Deuteronomy 8:11, 12, 14).

Know therefore that the Lord your God, He is God, the faithful God, who keeps His covenant and His lovingkindness to a thousandth generation with those who love Him and keep His commandments (Deuteronomy 7:9).

And now, Israel, what does the Lord your God require from you, but to fear the Lord your God, to walk in all His ways and love Him, and to serve the Lord your God with all your heart and with all your soul (Deuteronomy 10:12).

But the land into which you are about to cross to possess it, a land of hills and valleys, drinks water from the rain of heaven, a land for which the Lord your God cares; the eyes of the Lord your God are always on it, from the beginning even to the end of the year.

And it shall come about if you listen obediently to my commandments which I am commanding you today, to love the Lord your God and to serve Him with all your heart and all your soul, that He will give the rain for your land in its season, the early and late rain, that you may gather in your grain and your new wine and your oil. And He will give grass in your fields for your cattle, and you shall eat and be satisfied. Beware, lest your hearts be deceived and you turn away and serve other gods and worship them. Or the anger of the Lord will be kindled against you, and he will shut up the heavens so that there will be no rain and the ground will not yield its fruit; and you will perish quickly from the good land which the LORD is giving you (Deuteronomy 11:11-17 NASB1995).

During these 50 days—usually between mid-April and mid-June–the flowers of the olive, grape, pomegranate, and date open, and the embryonic figs begin to develop. The blossoms of these flowers permeate the hills and valleys with the sweetest smell. This fragrance is enough to draw any weary traveler to the vineyard and fields. The flower petals decorate the landscape like a bride prepares for her wedding.

During this same period the kernels of wheat and barley fill with starch. The fate of these 7 foods is determined during this 50-day period. Therefore, the fate of the nation is also determined during these 50 days because these are their basic crops for survival. Their very sustenance for life.

Those who have traveled to Israel during the spring know weather changes are inevitable. The winds vary from scorching southern winds to cold wet winds from the north and west.

The scorching southern winds bring with them extreme dryness and heat, while the northern winds darken the skies, generating tempestuous storms, with thunder, lightning, and rain.

And when you see a south wind blowing, you say, 'It will be a hot day,' and it turns out that way (Luke 12:55).

This delicate season is a direct provision by God. A reminder of his promises, provisions, and grace.

The northern winds blowing over Israel between Passover and Shavuot bring rain. This wind and rain is most beneficial to the wheat and barley because it is in the third stage of ripening.

But this same wind wreaks havoc on the olive, grapes, dates, and pomegranate crops if buds have already opened into flowers.

The north wind can be a blessing to the wheat when it has reached a third of its ripening and a curse to the olives if it comes after they have bloomed but before they have been pollinated.

On the other hand, a prolonged southern wind is good for the flower crops, but this wind can devastate the wheat and barley if it comes before the kernels have filled with starch, for then the grain will be scorched, and the crop decimated as described in Pharaoh's dream in Genesis 41:6

And behold there sprouted seven ears, thin and scorched by the southern east wind.

This delicate balance is controlled by God. The flowers of the olives, grapes, male dates, and pomegranates need successive days of dry heat and southern wind. Under ideal conditions these flowers open, allowing the pollen to reach the pistils for pollination.

But if the heat wave is too brief and pollination has not been completed before the cold northern wind comes, the flowers blow away by the wind or the pollen is washed off by the rain.

The perfect timing of the northern wet winds is necessary for the filling of the wheat and barley. The perfect timing of the warm southern winds is necessary for the fruition of the other trees.

He caused the east wind to blow in the heavens.
And by His power He directed the south wind (Psalm 78:26).

For behold, He who forms mountains and creates the wind
And declares to man what are His thoughts,
He who makes dawn into darkness
And treads on the high places of the earth,
The Lord God of hosts is His name (Amos 4:13).

For He spoke and raised up a stormy wind,
Which lifted up the waves of the sea (Psalm 107:25).

He causes the vapors to ascend from the ends of the earth;
Who makes lightnings for the rain,
Who brings forth the wind from His treasuries (Psalm 135:7).

PROMISES, PROVISIONS, AND GRACE REPLICATED IN THE TABERNACLE

The direction of the wind with the provision of these seven foods is symbolized in God's directive in the placements of the Tabernacle elements. The north winds for the fruition of the wheat is shown in the placement of the table of showbread in the north side of the tabernacle. The southern warm winds are necessary to the olive plants and are demonstrated by the placement of the menorah, lampstand lit with olive oil on the southern side.

And he will love you and bless you and multiply you; He will also bless the fruit of your womb and the fruit of your ground, your grain and your new wine and your oil, the increase of your herd and the young of your flock in the land which He swore to your forefathers to give you (Deuteronomy 7:13).

God desires to bless you.

Ask rain from the Lord at the time of the spring rain—The Lord who makes the storm clouds; and He will give them showers of rain, vegetation in the field of each man (Zechariah 10:1).

The wind, rain, and sun are directed by our Lord God. The one true God.

The pagans in the land were also aware of the wind, rain, sun, and storms. The worship of Baal was based on their belief he was the god of rain, thunder, lightning, and death.

Ray VanDer Laan writes this about the complexity facing the Israelites:

Baal's victory over death was thought to be repeated each year when he returned from the land of death (underworld), bringing rain to renew the earth's fertility. Hebrew culture viewed the sea as evil and destructive, so Baal's promise to prevent storms and control the sea, as well as his ability to produce harvests, made him attractive to the Israelites. It is hard to know why Yahweh's people failed to see that he alone had power over these things. Possibly, their desert origins led them to question God's sovereignty over fertile land. Or maybe it was simply the sinful pagan practices that attracted them to Baal. [8]

I found Israel like grapes in the wilderness; I saw your forefathers as the earliest fruit on the fig tree in its first season. But they came to Baal-peor and devoted themselves to shame, And they became as detestable as that which they loved (Hosea 9:10).

God was not surprised or delighted in the Israelites pattern of worship.

As a direct challenge to the Israelites' faith in Baal, who they worshiped as the "god of rain," God withheld rain and dew from the land for three years to prove that He alone was Creator and Lord (1 Kings 17:1).

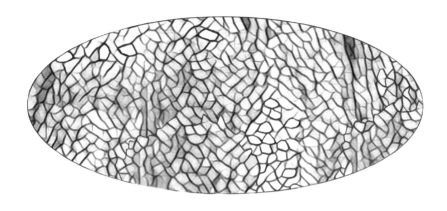

GRACE THAT SATISFIES

God uses every part of his creation to demonstrate grace and redemption to us. Redemption is the finality of his promises, provisions, and grace. It was more than the Israelites or us deserve. It is grace—unmerited favor.

The Israelites were headed into the pit of paganism as they entered the Promised Land. Moses diligently tried to prepare them and bring them to the belief and understanding that only the one true God is who they should serve. When they did not follow God's commands to clear the land of idols and those who worshiped the idols, their curiosity overcame them.

When the land was ripe for the harvest of wheat and barley they were to look to the one true God. Yet, their eyes wandered. Their minds were not satisfied as God requested. On another hillside, high on a mountain during the same 50 days, the pagans worshiped their gods. Child sacrifice and temple harlotry was at the highest peak.

Today, pagans of our land are dancing on the media altar serving fear, chaos, and uncertainty while celebrating the sacrifice of babies and destruction of women across our land. Families are being torn apart. Children are being dismembered.

God is not surprised or delighted.

Do you know the balances of the clouds, the wondrous works of him who is perfect in knowledge (Job 37:16 ESV).

We have a choice. Fear of the world or fear in awe of God. Fear of God is to stand firm on His promises, provisions, and grace and stand in awe.

Fear of the Lord is the fountain of life.

God's promises, "I will never leave you or forsake you." If you don't want to follow or give in to a command by an employer, because it will edify fetal tissue, then never forget, God is the ultimate provider. He is our sustainer.

Uncertainty is on many faces, yet knowing Christ as your Savior removes all uncertainty and lets us live in grace.

Will trouble come? Yes.

The Lord says, "My grace is sufficient for you."

God used these seven foods as a reminder every year of his promises, provisions, and grace. Every year their livelihood was dependent on these crops, therefore the rain, sun, wind, and heat. He wanted them to look to him—and be satisfied and content in him

God is still the same. He is in control, and he wants us to be content in him.

Delight yourself in the Lord and He will give you the desires of your heart (Psalm 37:4).

When we delight in the Lord, we are satisfied in him.

When we delight in ourselves, our pride leads to sin.

How do we continue to experience the flavors of His grace?

Remember the story of the old grandfather retelling how God delivered his family to the promised land? This is an example of what we need to do. Come to the table and fellowship, break bread together, and tell family members what God is doing in our lives, how he is answering prayers, providing, and demonstrating grace.

Our children need to know these stories. They need to live these stories. Even if they roll their eyes and say, "There goes dad again telling us how God helped him at work." or "There goes mom again, sharing how she witnessed at school and the teacher accepted Christ." We can teach our children as we walk along the road, as we rise up, and as we lay down. When they know the stories of how God has worked in our life better than we can tell it ourselves, then we have done well.

If you say you don't have any stories, start praying for God to show you His promises, provisions, and grace. Then share with everyone what he is doing.

Enjoy the foods God delivered to us and avoid the lab experiments of man. Your body knows the difference and talks to you. Eat God's foods and your body returns the favor with energy and emotional well being. Eat man's foods and your body speaks with complaints of pain, inflammation, and depression.

Learn to savor the flavors of His grace. Learn to be satisfied in His provisions and not look elsewhere. Food can become the overindulgence gods of our day. The god of gluttony. The god of obesity. The god of apathetic attention to God's desires.

Food evokes memories, and memories are a reminder of God's grace. Grace of yesterday is the same grace available to us today. Grace is an attribute of God, and God never changes.

As I prepare meals with wheat, barley, figs, dates, pomegranate, grapes, and olives, I teach my family the true story of grace. It thrills my heart to see these verses we have covered in this book and see all the ways God has blessed us with his provisions, promises, and grace. Grace that satisfies.

Let every meal tell a story of God's promises, provisions and grace.

And as the verse in Deuteronomy 8:10 ends, "When you have eaten and are satisfied, you shall bless the Lord your God for the good land which he has given you." We get to celebrate in that promise. We too can serve these seven foods to our family and share the story of His promises.

The fruits of the land depend on him—sun, wind, rain, and heat.

The fruits of our lives depend on him—guidance, provisions, and love

The flavors of grace satisfy.

Are you ready to experience more grace?

Are you ready to teach your family about grace?

PART 3

RECIPES

Wheat

1 SAMUEL 6:13

Now the people of Beth-shemesh were reaping their wheat harvest in the valley, and they raised their eyes and saw the ark and were glad to see it.

PSALM 147:14

He makes peace in your borders; He satisfies you with the finest of the wheat.

JOHN 12:24

Truly, Truly, I say to you, unless a grain of wheat falls into th earth and dies, it remains by itself alone, but if it dies, it bears much fruit.

LUKE 22: 31-32

Simon, Simon, behold, Satan has demanded permission to sift ou like wheat; but I have prayed for you that your faith may not fail; and you when once you have turned again, strengthen your brothers.

MATTHEW 13:24-30

He presented another parable to them, saying, "The kingdom of heaven may be compared to a man who sowed good seed in his field, "But while men were sleeping, his enemy came and sowed tares also among the wheat, and went away.

"But when the wheat sprang up and bore grain, then the tares became evident also,

"And the slaves of the land owner came and said to him, 'Sir, did you not sow good seed in your field? How then does it have tares?'

"And he said to them, 'An enemy has done this!' And the slaves said to him, 'Do you want us, then, to go and gather them up?'

"But he said, 'No, lest while you are gathering up the tares, you may root up the wheat with them.'

"'Allow both to grow together until the harvest; and in the time of the harvest I will say to the reapers, First gather up the tares and bind them in bundles to burn them up but gather the wheat into my barn.'"

Toasted Grain

JOSHUA 5:11

1 pound whole wheat kernels – hard or soft, or other varieties

1 teaspoon salt

1 teaspoon olive oil or water

Heat a frying pan and pour in the seeds and salt. Stir constantly until lightly browned. Sprinkle a little water over while toasting, to soften the seeds. Eat as you would popcorn.

RECIPE FROM *FOOD AT THE TIME OF THE BIBLE,* MIRIAM VAMOSH.

Unleavened Bread
Exodus 12:39

2 cups freshly milled whole wheat flour; any variety will be delicious such as einkorn, spelt, hard red, hard white, and kamut
¾ cup cold water
2 tablespoons olive oil
1 teaspoon salt
Additional flavorings: rosemary, onion, garlic, sesame seeds, sumac, za'atar

Combine the flour, olive oil and salt with the water to form a dough and knead for 3 minutes.

When kneading the dough, pray for those who need a Savior or are hurting.

Add chosen flavorings. My favorites are garlic and onion. But I have been experimenting more with za'atar.

Divide dough into 8 pieces. Flatten each into a thin round and prick with a fork. Cook individually on a hot griddle or in the oven at 500° for 10 minutes.

Sprouted Wheat Berries

Sprouting whole organic grains increases vitamin content and for some people is easier to digest. Sprouting whole grains has shown to increase Vitamin E by as much as 300 times. The seeds, which are already a living organism when the germ is intact, become more alive when the germination takes place. The exposed enzymes are now catalysts and aid in digestion, neutralize toxins, cleanse the blood and provide energy.

> 1 cup organic wheat berries: wheat, spelt, kamut, emmer, einkorn, or rye
> Water

Soak one cup of berries in a container filled with water for 24 hours.

Strain the water and save it in a bottle for drinking.

Replace the container cap with a screen material fastened with a thick rubber band to facilitate rinsing and drainage. Keep your container slightly slanted horizontally so that any excess water can drain out into your kitchen sink.

Rinse the sprouts in water and drain well daily.

In three days your sprouts are ready. The sprouts are ready when the tail is ¼ to ½ inch long. Make sure to rinse and refrigerate or use before wheatgrass begins to grow or it will be hard and chewy.

Use the wheat sprouts in salads, casseroles, stir-fires, breads and cakes.

Or make this your new chewing gum!

Barley

JOHN 6:9

There is a lad here who has five barley loaves and two fish, but what are these for so many people?

JOHN 6:10 - 14

Jesus said, "Have the people sit down, "Not there was much grass in the place. So the men sat down, in number about five thousand.

Jesus therefore took the loaves; and having given thanks, He distributed to those who were seated; likewise also of the fish as much as they wanted.

And when they were filled, He said to His disciples, "Gather up the left-over fragments that nothing may be lost."

And so they gathered them up, and filled the twelve baskets with fragments from the five barley loaves, which were left over by those who had eaten.

When therefore the people saw the sign which He had performed, they said, "this is of a truth the Prophet who is to come into the world."

RUTH 1:21

So Naomi returned, and with her Ruth the Moabitess, her daughter-in-law, who returned from the land of Moab. And they came to Bethlehem at the beginning of barley harvest.

2 KINGS 4:42

Now a man came from Ballshalishad, and brought the man of God bread fo the the first fruits, twenty loaves of barley and fresh ears of grain in his sack. And he said "give them to the people that they may eat."

JEREMIAH 41:8

But ten men who were found among them said to Ishmael, "Do not put us to death; for we have stores of wheat, barley, oil and honey hidden in the field." So he refrained and did not put them to death along with their companions.

Mediterranean Barley Salad

1½ cups pearl barley

1 tablespoon salt plus ½ teaspoon

½ teaspoon pepper

3 tablespoons olive oil

2 tablespoons pomegranate molasses (see recipe in this book)

½ teaspoon cinnamon

¼ teaspoon cumin

⅓ cup currants

½ cup coarsely chopped cilantro

¼ cup nuts—pecans or pistachios, toasted and chopped coarsely

3 ounces feta, crumbled

6 scallions; green parts only, sliced thinly

½ cup pomegranate seeds

Bring 4 quarts of water to boil. Add barley and 1 tablespoon salt. Cook until tender for 20-40 minutes. Drain, spread onto a rimmed baking sheet and let cool completely. About 15 minutes

Whisk oil, molasses, cinnamon, cumin and ½ teaspoon salt together in a bowl. Add barley, currants, cilantro, and nuts. Gently toss to combine. Season with salt and pepper to taste.

Spread barley salad evenly on a platter; arrange feta, scallions, and pomegranate seeds in separate diagonal rows on top. Drizzle with additional oil and serve.

Barley Pilaf

4 servings

2 tablespoons olive oil

1 onion finely chopped

1 sweet red pepper, seeded and finely diced; substitute green or yellow peppers

¾ cup pearl barley

1½ cups beef broth; substitute chicken or vegetable broth

Heat the oil in a medium skillet, and sauté the onion and pepper until softened. Add the barley and sauté 1 minute more.

In a medium saucepan, bring the broth to a boil and then add the barley.

Cook over medium-low heat until bubbly. Continue until all broth is absorbed and barley is tender. If more liquid is required, add in broth or water 2 tablespoons at a time. Watch closely so there is no burning or scorching.

The pilaf can be made ahead and reheated in the microwave or air fryer for about 5 minutes.

Apple Cinnamon Barley Pudding

A delicious similarity to rice pudding and tapioca pudding, only a much chewier version!

6¼ cups whole milk or nut milk, my favorite is homemade almond milk

3 tablespoons organic butter, coconut oil can be substituted

2 apples peeled and diced, use organic to include the peeling

¾ cup pearl barley

¼ cup organic raisins; substitute cranberries or currants

1 teaspoon ground cinnamon

¼ tsp salt (I use Redmond's Real Salt)

½ cup pure maple syrup, honey can be substituted

¼ cup organic heavy cream: substitute sour cream or plain yogurt

Ground cinnamon for topping

In a medium saucepan, bring the milk to a slow simmer over medium heat.

Meanwhile, melt the butter in a large skillet or sauté pan set over medium-low heat; add the apples and barley and stir until the grains of barley are well coated and slightly toasted, about 3 minutes.

Stir in raisins, cinnamon and salt, then start adding the warm milk, about 1 cup or so at a time. Continue to stir constantly, making sure that the milk is completely absorbed before adding more. Continue stirring and adding milk until the barley is tender and creamy, which should take about 55 minutes from the time you first started adding milk. It is particularly important that you never stop stirring; otherwise the milk might scorch, curdle and/or stick to the bottom of the pan.

Toward the end, taste regularly to gauge the doneness of the barley; you may not need to use all the milk, or you may need a little more, depending on how soft you like your pudding.

Once the barley is cooked to your desire, stir in a final cup of warm milk as well as the maple syrup, turn off the heat and let the pudding rest, stirring from time to time, until it's thickened and cooled to the desired serving temperature, about 45 -60 minutes.

Stir in heavy cream, if using. If you prefer your pudding a bit on the colder side, you can set it in the refrigerator for a quick cool.

Serve topped with a dollop of whipped heavy cream, sour cream or plain yogurt, with a few drops of maple syrup. Then garnish with a sprinkle of cinnamon and cranberries.

Leftovers will keep in the refrigerator for up to a few days, but the pudding will become fairly thick and pasty once chilled. Reheat for a few seconds in the microwave to make it creamy again, or, if serving cold, stir in a little bit of milk to loosen it up

Beany Barley Salad
6 servings

½ cup pearl barley

½ cup jasmine rice, or brown rice

1 cup black beans cooked, drained

1 cup kidney beans, cooked, drained

1 cup organic corn kernels, cooked

½ cup chopped green onions

1 red or green pepper, chopped

¼ cup fresh cilantro, chopped

8 Romaine lettuce leaves

¼ cup pomegranate balsamic vinegar; substitute red wine vinegar

1 clove garlic, minced

1 teaspoon chili powder

½ teaspoon salt

¼ teaspoon freshly ground black pepper

½ cup olive oil

In a large saucepan bring 2 cups of water to a boil. Stir in barley and reduce heat to medium-low, cover and simmer for 40 to 45 minutes or until tender. Let cool.

In a saucepan bring 1½ cups water to a boil, add the rice. Reduce heat to low and simmer, covered for about 20 minutes or until tender. Let cool.

In a large bowl, combine the cooled barley, rice, black beans, kidney beans, corn, onions, red bell pepper and cilantro. Mix well.

Dressing: In a small bowl, whisk together vinegar, garlic, chili powder, salt, and black pepper. Whisk in oil and pour over salad and toss well. Transfer to a lettuce-lined bowl to serve.

Grapes

Numbers 13:21-23

So they went up and spied out the land from the wilderness of Zin as far as Rehob, at Lebo-hamath. When they had gone up into the Negev, they came to Hebron where Ahiman, Sheshai, and Talmai, the descendants of Anak were. (Now Hebron was built seven years before Zoan in Egypt.)

Then they came to the valley of Eshcol and from there cut down a branch with a single cluster of grapes; and they carried it on a pole between two men, with some of the pomegranates and the figs.

Deuteronomy 28:39

You shall plant and cultivate vineyards, but you shall neither drink of the wine nor gather the grapes, for the worm shall devour them.

Leviticus 26:5

Indeed, your threshing will last for you until grape gathering, and grape gathering will last until sowing time. You will thus eat your food to the full and live securely in your land.

Isaiah 62:8-9

The Lord has sworn by His right hand and by His strong arm, I will never again give your grain as food for your enemies; Now will foreigners drink your new wine, for which you have labored."

But those who garner it will eat it, and praise the Lord: And those who gather it will drink it in the courts of My sanctuary.

Frozen Yogurt Bites

1 pound grapes – organic is best option

1 cup organic yogurt

TOPPINGS:

Crushed granola, coconut, finely chopped nuts or chia seeds

Line a cookie sheet with parchment paper. Using a toothpick, dip each grape dip into the yogurt. Then dip into the topping of choice. Set each grape on the cookie sheet. Place the cookie sheet in the freezer.

Once completely frozen – serve anytime for a delicious delight.

Grape Honey

4 cups grapes

½ cup water

Wash grapes and remove stems. Place grapes in a pan with water. Boil about 20 minutes over medium heat or until mixture thickens. Strain off any remaining grape seeds. For a creamy texture blend for a few seconds in a blender.

Store in sterilized jars and refrigerate.

The natural sugars in the grapes are concentrated when the grapes are boiled down to a pulpy syrup.

Key – the sweeter the grapes, the sweeter the honey.

7 Species Labneh

Recipe contributed by Artza in Israel
A perfect dessert or sweet appetizer. It was a hit!

3⅓ cup plain organic yogurt

½ teaspoon sea salt

6 grapes, cut in half

3 fresh figs, cut in quarters

handful pomegranate seeds

1 tablespoon silan; silan is a date honey. Grape honey or pomegranate molasses can be used.

handful crushed walnuts

Start by making yo-cheese.

Strain the yogurt.

Place a strainer over a bowl.

Place a cheese cloth or tea towel over strainer.

An alternative to the bowl and cheesecloth is a Yogurt Cheese Maker produced by Cuisipro

Mix together the yogurt and salt

Pour yogurt and salt mixture over cheesecloth.

Wrap cheese cloth over the yogurt and place a weight over it (you can use anything in your fridge!)

Place in fridge for 4-6 hours (or until it reaches a cream cheese texture)

Scoop out cheese amd mix with silan

Spread cheese mixture into a serving bowl

Top with fruit and nuts.

Be'teavon בתאבון (enjoy!)

Figs

MATTHEW 24:32

Now learn the parable from the fig tree; when its branch has already become tender, and puts forth its leaves, you know that summer is near.

MARK 11:11-14

And He entered Jerusalem and came into the temple; and after looking all around, He departed for Bethany with the twelve, since it was already late.

And on the next day, when they had departed from Bethany He became hungry.

And seeing at a distance a fig tree in leaf, He went to see if perhaps He would find anything on it; and when He came to it, He found nothing but leaves, for it was not the season for figs.

And He answered and said to it, May no one ever eat fruit from you again!" And His disciples were listening.

LUKE 13:6-9

And He began telling this parable: "A man had a fig tree which had been planted in his vineyard; and he came looking for fruit on it and did not find any.

"And he said to the vineyard-keeper, 'Behold, for three years I have come looking for fruit on this fig tree without finding any. Cut it down! Why does it even use up the ground?'

"And he answered and said to him, 'Let it alone, sir, for this year too, until I dig around it and put in fertilizer; and if it bears fruit next year, fine; but if not, cut it down.'

REVELATION 6:13

And the stars of the sky fell to the earth, as a fig tree casts its unripe figs when shaken by a great wind.

1 KINGS 4:25

So Judah and Israel lived in safety, every man under his vine and his fig tree, from Dan even to Beersheba, all the days of Solomon.

Fig Cake

3 eggs, lightly beaten

1 cup olive oil

1 cup buttermilk; substitute nut milk, but it does best with buttermilk

1 teaspoon vanilla

2 cups freshly milled flour; spelt, kamut and hard white are best

1½ cups organic sugar, less is ok, or sucanat

1 teaspoon salt

1 teaspoon baking soda

1 teaspoon cinnamon

1 teaspoon nutmeg

½ teaspoon cloves

1½ cups chopped fresh figs; substitute fig preserves

½ cup chopped pecans

Mix dry ingredients completely with a whisk or a Fiskie, my favorite kitchen tool. See my website for this fun tool. Then add in wet ingredients and mix thoroughly.

Fold in pecans and figs.

Pour into a greased and floured bundt pan. A 9 inch round baking pan can also be used.

Bake at 350° for approx. 30 to 35 min. Check to see if it is done by using a toothpick. If done, the toothpick will come out clean.

Baking may take up to 45 minutes to complete.

Buttermilk Glaze

½ cup buttermilk

1 cup organic sugar

½ cup butter

1 tablespoon pomegranate molasses (see recipe on page 137)

1 teaspoon vanilla

Bring all ingredients to a rolling boil and cook for 3 minutes. Allow glaze to cool before drizzling over cake. Use a toothpick to poke holes in the cake, so glaze can go down into it.

Apple-Fig Crumble
Makes 8 servings

1 cup chopped dried figs

3 tablespoons apple juice – or more if needed

3 large tart, crisp apples, peeled, cored, cut into thick slices; can use apples with peelings if using organic apples and they are washed well

1 tablespoon fresh milled flour; soft white wheat flour or spelt is perfect

¼ teaspoon cinnamon

2 tablespoons honey, agave or maple syrup

1 tablespoon butter

Topping

⅔ cup fresh milled flour

⅔ cup sucanat or organic sugar

½ teaspoon cinnamon

⅛ teaspoon salt

6 tablespoons butter, cut into ½ inch pieces

Heat oven to 350°F.

Coat an 8 x 8-inch baking dish with an organic cooking spray.

Place figs and apple juice in a saucepan and cook for 2 minutes on medium heat. Turn down to simmer until juice is absorbed. Let stand for 5 minutes. Stir until most of the liquid is absorbed. Set aside.

Place apples in the prepared baking dish. Sprinkle top with flour and cinnamon, toss to coat. Heat honey and butter until melted; drizzle over apples.

Arrange figs over apples.

For topping combine flour, sucanat, cinnamon and salt in a medium bowl; cut in butter until crumbly. Sprinkle over apples and figs.

Bake for 40 minutes or until the topping is golden brown and the filling is bubbly. Serve warm.

Broccoli Fig Salad

1 cup stemmed and finely chopped figs

1½ pounds broccoli, florets cut into 1-inch pieces, stalks peeled and sliced ¼ inch thick

½ cup plain organic yogurt

1 tablespoon balsamic vinegar

½ teaspoon salt

1 teaspoon pepper

½ cup walnuts, toasted and coarsely chopped

1 large shallot, minced or 4 green onions

Combine 4 cups water and 4 cups ice in a large bowl.

Bring 3 quarts of water to boil in Dutch oven or medium pot. Remove 1 cup boiling water and combine with figs in a small bowl; cover, let sit for 5 minutes, and drain.

Meanwhile, add broccoli stalks to boiling water and cook for 1 minute. Add florets and cook until slightly tender, about 1 minute. Drain broccoli and place in ice water to cool. Drain again, transfer to salad spinner and spin dry.

Whisk yogurt, vinegar, ½ teaspoon salt and 1 teaspoon pepper together in a large bowl. Add broccoli, drained figs, walnuts and shallots to bowl with dressing and toss to combine. Season with salt and pepper to taste.

Figs Stuffed with Goat Cheese

1½ ounces goat cheese

8 fresh figs, halved lengthwise

16 walnut halves, toasted; substitute pecan halves

3 tablespoons honey or maple syrup

Heat oven to 500° F.

Spoon heaping ½ teaspoon goat cheese onto each fig half and arrange in a parchment paper lined baking sheet.

Bake figs until heated through, about 4 minutes.

Transfer figs to a serving platter.

Place 1 nut half on top of each fig and drizzle with honey or maple syrup.

Serve immediately.

Pomegranates

EXODUS 39:24

They made pomegranates of blue and purple and scarlet material and twisted linen on the hem of the robe.

NUMBERS 20:5

Why have you made us come up from Egypt, to bring us into this wretched place? It is not a place of grain or figs or vines or pomegranates, nor is there water to drink.

1 KINGS 7:18

So he made the pillars, and two rows around on the one network to cover the capitals which were on the top of the pomegranates; and so he did for the other capital.

SONG OF SOLOMON 6:11

I went down to the orchard of nut trees

To see the blossoms of the valley,

To see whether the vine had budded

Or the pomegranates had bloomed.

Easy Pomegranate Smoothie

Yield: 1 large or 2 small

A power drink with flavor, nutrients, and protein.

1 cup pomegranate seeds (cut and seed 1 pomegranate or buy 5 ounces seeds)

1 whole pitted date

1 cup frozen pineapple chunks

½ teaspoon cinnamon

1 teaspoon chia seeds

1 banana, frozen or room temperature

⅓ cup Greek yogurt

Stevia if more sweetness is desired

Place the pomegranate seeds and date in the blender and blend for a few seconds until mostly liquefied.

Add the remaining ingredients in the blender. Blend until creamy and frothy, stopping and scraping down the sides as necessary.

Enjoy immediately or store 1 day in a sealed jar; if it separates, shake to re-integrate it

Pomegranate Molasses

Makes ⅔ cup

This sauce can be used in all sweet recipes, vinaigrettes and syrup for topping your favorite pancakes or yogurt.

2 tablespoons water

1 tablespoon organic sugar

4 cups unsweetened pomegranate juice (no additives or added ingredients)

2 teaspoons lemon juice – freshly squeezed will liven up the sauce, yet from a jar is ok.

Combine the water and sugar in a medium saucepan until completely moistened. Bring to boil and cook until sugar begins to turn golden; 2-3 minutes. Be careful not to scorch the sauce. Cook 1 minute more.

This becomes a caramel like sauce in the color of mahogany brown.

Carefully add in 2 tablespoons of pomegranate juice until incorporated; mixture will bubble and steam. Slowly whisk in the remaining pomegranate juice and lemon juice, scraping up any caramel.

Bring mixture to light boil then turn heat to medium and cook until mixture sticks to the back of a spoon.

Festive Pomegranate Salad

⅓ pound arugula

1 small head red leaf lettuce

½ cup pomegranate seeds

½ cup walnut pieces, toasted

1 avocado, diced

½ cup feta cheese, crumbled

3 medium beets cooked, diced and chilled

Tear the arugula and red leaf lettuce into pieces and place in a large bowl. Add beets and all remaining salad ingredients. Immediately before serving add the Pomegranate Citrus Vinaigrette and toss.

Pomegranate Citrus Vinaigrette
Makes enough for more than one salad.

½ cup olive oil

2 cloves of garlic, minced

2 green onions, finely diced

1 orange, juiced

1 tablespoon lemon juice

¼ cup red wine vinegar

1 tablespoon balsamic vinegar

2 tablespoons pomegranate molasses (see recipe in this book)

1 teaspoon salt

¼ teaspoon pepper

1 teaspoon organic sugar – optional

Add all ingredients into a blender or food processor. Blend until smooth.

Store in an airtight dressing bottle. Enjoy and share the story of the 7 foods at the table.

Chocolate Pomegranate Bites

This is the perfect holiday treat! The burst of juice in the chocolate will surprise and delight your guests.

Two ingredients or more if you like options.

> 1 bag (12 ounces) of dark chocolate chips, prefer 70% or higher for nutritional value
>
> 1 cup pomegranate seeds, patted dry
>
> ¼ cup chopped walnuts or pecans – optional
>
> ¼ cup unsweetened coconut – optional
>
> ¼ teaspoon cinnamon - optional

In a microwave or on the stove top, melt dark chocolate chips; stir until smooth. Remove from the stove. Stir in pomegranate seeds and optional ingredients.

Drop by tablespoons onto waxed paper-lined baking sheets. Or use mini muffin liners for a more festive look.

Refrigerate until firm, about 1 hour. Store between layers of waxed paper in an airtight container in the refrigerator.

Olives

EXODUS **27:20**

You shall charge the sons of Israel, that they bring you clear oil of beaten olives for the light, to make a lamp burn continually.

ISAIAH **17:6**

Yet gleanings will be left in it like the shaking of an olive tree,

Two or three olives on the topmost bough,

Four or five on the branches of a fruitful tree,

Declares the Lord, the God of Israel.

JAMES **3:12**

Can a fig tree, my brethren, produce olives, or a vine produce figs? Nor can salt water produce fresh.

LUKE **19:37**

As soon as He was approaching, near the descent of the Mount of Olives, the whole crowd of the disciples began to praise God joyfully with a loud voice for all the miracles which they had seen.

Spaghetti with Figs, Lemons and Olive Oil

1 pound spaghetti

Salt and pepper

¼ cup extra-virgin olive oil, plus extra for serving

1 shallot, minced equal to 3 tablespoons

¼ cup organic heavy cream

1 cup finely chopped dried figs; fresh figs are also very good

¼ cup sliced olives; optional

2 teaspoons finely grated lemon zest plus ¼ cup juice; 2 lemons is typical

½ cup parmesan cheese, plus extra for serving

2 tablespoons shredded fresh basil

Bring 4 quarts of water to boil in a large Dutch oven.

Add pasta and 1 tablespoon salt to the boiling water and cook, stirring often, until al dente. Reserve 1¾ cups cooking water, then drain pasta in a colander and set aside.

Heat 1 tablespoon of oil in an empty pot over medium heat until it shimmers. Add shallot and 1 teaspoon salt, cook until shallot is softened, about 2 minutes. Whisk 1½ cup reserved cooking water and cream into pot; add figs and olives; stir to combine.

Bring to a simmer and cook for 2 minutes. Remove pot from heat, add pasta and stir until coated. Stir in remaining 3 tablespoons oil, lemon zest and juice, parmesan and 1 teaspoon pepper.

Cover and let pasta stand for 2 minutes, tossing frequently and adding remaining ½ cup reserved cooking water as needed to adjust consistency. Stir in basil and season with salt and pepper to taste. Serve with extra parmesan cheese.

Roasted Feta Cheese and Olive Oil

Recipe inspired by *The Complete Mediterranean Cookbook*

2, 8-ounce blocks feta cheese, sliced into ½ inch slabs

¼ teaspoon red pepper flakes

¼ teaspoon fresh cracked pepper

2 tablespoons olive oil

2 teaspoons minced fresh parsley

The feta cheese is going to be broiled. Place the oven rack 4 inches from the broiler element. Or use an Air Fryer or Smart Oven. Pat feta cheese dry with paper towels and arrange on a broiler safe dish.

Sprinkle it with red pepper flakes and pepper. Broil until edges of cheese are golden, 3 to 8 minutes. Keep a sharp eye on it so there is no burning.

Drizzle with oil, sprinkle with parsley, and serve immediately.

Can be served on tortillas, bread, lettuce leaf, sliced tomatoes or by itself.

Olive Oil Garlic Mayo

Recipe makes 1 cup.

With a blender and a steady hand you will have delicious homemade mayo in minutes!

1 whole egg plus 1 egg yolk

2 tablespoons red wine vinegar

½ teaspoon dry mustard

½ teaspoon salt

¼ teaspoon white pepper

1 clove garlic, minced

¾ to 1 cup olive oil

Put the eggs in a blender. With the blender running, add the vinegar, spices and garlic, one at a time, through the feed tube in the lid and blend until the garlic is pureed.

With the blender running add the oil in a slow, steady stream through the feed tube until the mayo is thick and will incorporate no more oil.

To store, use a just cleaned jar and lid – preferably removed from a hot sudsy wash or the dishwasher. No bacteria can be in the jar. Add the mayo to a dry perfectly clean jar. Mayo will keep for up to 2 weeks. It probably won't last that long since the flavor is so fresh and amazing.

Olive Oil Dipping Sauce

This is perfect for Unleavened Bread, Fresh Milled Whole Wheat bread and also the Jerusalem Flat Bread.

For every 8 ounces of olive oil add your choice of these ingredients:

- Rosemary

- Hyssop

- Thyme

- Garlic – 1 clove whole or minced

- Za'atar – 1 teaspoon

Store in a glass jar with a tight fitting lid. Place in a cool dry place or in the refrigerator. When it is served I also add finely grated parmesan cheese.

Dates

2 SAMUEL 6:19

Further, he distributed to all the people, to all the multitude of Israel, both to men and women, a cake of bread and one of dates and one of raisins to each one. Then all the people departed each to his house.

SONG OF SOLOMON 5:11

His head is like gold, pure gold; His locks are like clusters of dates

And black as a raven.

EXODUS 3:8

So I have come down to deliver them from the power of the Egyptians, and to bring them up from that land to a good and spacious land, to a land flowing with milk and honey, to the place of the Canaanite and the Hittite and the Amorite and the Perizzite and the Hivite and the Jebusite.

EXODUS 16:31

The house of Israel named it manna, and it was like coriander seed, white, and its taste was like wafers with honey.

BAKED FRUIT DELIGHT

Serves 10

Recipe inspired by Robin Jeep from the book *Antioxidant Diet.*

Another all-time favorite – serve for breakfast, lunch, dinner or pleasure! Hot or cold!

Can be served as is or as a topping on a fresh bed of favorite greens. I have also served this over quinoa.

6 apples, chopped

8 dates, chopped

1 cup currants or chopped fresh (or dried) figs

1 cup frozen cherries

1 cup frozen blueberries

1 cup crushed pineapple with juice

¼ cup water

¾ cup chopped walnuts or pecans

½ teaspoon cinnamon

¼ teaspoon nutmeg

Juice of one orange

2 teaspoons lemon zest

Preheat oven to 350 degrees.

Mix all ingredients. Put in a 9 x 13 baking dish and bake for 30 minutes or until all fruit is soft.

Great served warm or cold with Strawberry Topping.

NOTE: Currants seem to be harder to find so raisins can be substituted. Currants are the best option though.

STRAWBERRY TOPPING
Serves 8-10

½ cup almond milk

¼ cup cashew nuts

6 ounces frozen strawberries – thawed

2 dates, whole pitted

Blend all ingredients in a food processor until smooth and creamy.

The Ultimate Date Bar

1½ cup butter, melted, then cooled

1 cup date paste, or 1½ cups chopped dates

1½ cups walnuts, chopped

1 cup pecans, chopped (optional)

2 cup freshly milled flour; any variety will be perfect

½ teaspoon salt

½ teaspoon baking powder

¼ teaspoon baking soda

1 cup honey or grape honey,

4 eggs, set out at room temperature

1 teaspoon vanilla

Preheat your oven to 350° F.

Brush your pan with 2 tablespoons of the melted butter (one 9x13 pan or two 8x8 pans), making sure to grease the sides as well.

Mix with a whisk the flour, salt, baking powder and baking soda into a bowl. Set aside.

Add in the remaining 1¼ cup melted butter and honey until well incorporated. Add the eggs one at a time, mixing well after each addition. Add in the vanilla.

Mix in the flour mixture with the wet ingredients. Do this gently, by hand, until just incorporated.

Fold in the nuts with the batter.

Pour the batter (it will be very thick) onto the buttered pan(s).

Bake for 30 or more minutes, until light golden brown. It can take up to 40 or more minutes to cook, so keep checking. The bars are done when a toothpick inserted in the center comes out with moist crumbs.

Let cool, and cut into squares or bars.

Store these in an airtight container. They will stay moist if wrapped tightly.

Date Paste

Many recipes can use date paste in place of sugar.

    1 pound Medjool dates, pitted (about 2 cups tightly packed)

    1/2 cup water

In the bowl of a large food processor fitted with an "S" blade, combine the pitted dates and water.

Process until very smooth, scraping down the bowl to make sure all of the dates are incorporated.

Store the date paste in an airtight container in the fridge for up to two weeks, and use it in your favorite healthy recipes.

Whisk it into salad dressings to help emulsify and add a hint of sweetness. Swirl it into morning oatmeal. Sweeten a smoothie or fruit-based nice cream. Add it to soups, stews, chili's, or sauces that need a bit of sweetness.

Store date paste in an airtight container in the refrigerator for one month. It can technically store longer but it will begin to dry out. The date paste can also be frozen in a freezer safe airtight container.

Sephardic Charoset

2 cups date paste (see recipe on facing page)

1 cup walnuts, chopped

2 apples, peeled and chopped

½ teaspoon cinnamon

½ teaspoon cardamom – optional

2 tablespoon pomegranate molasses (see recipe on page 137)

So delicious you may want to double the batch before it disappears.

Blend all ingredients in a bowl and chill until ready to serve.

Makes the perfect topping on crackers as an appetizer or served on ice cream or yogurt.

Promised Land Salad
7 Species Salad

3 cups cooked barley or Israeli couscous

¼ cup dried chopped figs

¼ cup pitted dates, chopped

¼ cup halved grapes

¼ cup pomegranate seeds

¼ cup olive oil

2 teaspoon honey

2 teaspoon red wine vinegar or pomegranate vinegar

1 teaspoon honey mustard

¼ wheat/barley cereal – crunch grape nuts

2 tablespoon freshly chopped parsley leaves

Combine barley, figs, dates, grapes, and pomegranate seeds in a large bowl.

Place oil, honey, vinegar and mustard in a small bowl and whisk.

Pour dressing over barley and toss to coat.

Just before serving add cereal and toss to distribute. Garnish with parsley.

Acknowledgments

Recipe Image Contributors

These ladies from the Biblical Nutrition Academy Inner Circle, all enjoyed making and testing these recipes. They submitted the beutiful images in this book.

Audrey Gillies

Beth Lee

Debi Giordany

Denise Farrar

Janis Thomas

Kathy Barnes

Tina Chrismon

Ursula Gisler

Meet the Author

Health is taught all around us, but often not with the biblical insight. **Annette Reeder** delivers a fresh biblical perspective on how the Scriptures and nutrition intimately coincide. Her passion for the gift of health and nutrition makes getting healthy as a Christian a satisfying journey. Her desire and enthusiasm for this topic will bring motivation and eagerness to the reader, not only in eating, but in their personal relationship with God himself.

Annette Reeder is The Biblical Nutritionist on YouTube and has shared the message of God's love and food to more than 15 million viewers. Her academy, Biblical Nutrition Academy, has taught more than six thousand people how to live out God's recipe for excellent health.

And, as Annette will tell you often, "Just as we are physical, we are spiritual. And just as we are spiritual, we are physical. There is no separating the two."

In this powerful message, she delivers how God's food brings together fellowship, nourishment and satisfaction.

Annette Reeder has written more than 11 books on nutrition, including the bestselling healthy living Bible study: *Treasures of Healthy Living Bible Study.* Her cookbooks *Healthy Treasures Cookbook* and *Satisfied - Baking with Whole Grains* are top sellers for those who desire to eat real food from a loving God.

ENDNOTES

1 https://www.theatlantic.com/science/archive/2018/08/wheat-genome-is-best-thing-since-sliced-bread/567673/

2 https://bible.knowing-Jesus.com//topics/Grapes.

3 https://www.sciencedirect.com/science/article/pii/S0753332221009483

4 draxe.com/nutrition/pomegranate-seeds.

5 Henry, Matthew. 1706. Matthew Henry Commentary on the Whole Bible (Complete)

6 The Food and Feasts of Jesus, Douglas E. Neel and Joel A Pugh

7 http://penelope.uchicago.edu/josephus/ant-15.html: Josephus Book of Anitquities, Book XV, chapter IV, paragraph 2: Israel was God's vineyard on a hillside.

8 https://www.thattheworldmayknow.com/gates-of-hell-article